C000205134

WAR BOOK OF THE
GERMAN GENERAL STAFF

WAR BOOK OF THE
GERMAN GENERAL STAFF

GROSSGENERALSTAB

TRANSLATED WITH CRITICAL NOTES

BY

J. H. MORGAN

STACKPOLE
BOOKS

Stackpole Books © 2005

Cover design by Wendy Reynolds

Printed in the United States of America

Library of Congress Cataloging-in-Publication Data

Prussia (Kingdom). Armee. Grosser Generalstab.
  [Kriegsbrauch im Landkriege. English]
  War book of the German General Staff / Grossgeneralstab ;
translated with critical notes by J.H. Morgan.
      p. cm.
  Includes index.
  Originally published: 1915.
  ISBN 0-8117-0147-6 (alk. paper)
  1. War (International law) 2. World War, 1914–1918—
Law and legislation—Germany. I. Morgan, J. H. (John Hartman),
1876–1955. II. Title.

KZ6427.P78 2005
341.6'3'09041—dc22

2005015039

ISBN: 978-0-8117-0147-1

TABLE OF CONTENTS

FOREWORD

As we approach the 100th anniversary of World War I—the Great War, The War to End All Wars— we might look back at how the belligerents regarded warfare from their national perspectives. Each European country had a military strategy for defense of its homeland that was supposedly influenced by the customs and laws of war agreed to by the civilized nations of the world in various international agreements. Each country had laws-of-war books that synthesized the provisions of the agreements that were designed to guide the military commander's actions in combat. The war books told the commander what actions were acceptable, and what military actions were not acceptable.

The *War Book of the German General Staff* was just such a rule book. Its title was coined in 1915 by Professor J. H. Morgan of University College, London. The *War Book* is an Imperial German General Staff *(Grossgeneralstab)* publication titled *Kriegsbrauch im Landkriege*, which is translated as "Usage of War on Land" or more commonly, "Customs of Land Warfare." In 1902 when the book was published, there was very little "law" of land warfare.

The *War Book* was the official Imperial German General Staff handbook on the laws and customs of land warfare as they were known and interpreted by the German General Staff. Its purpose was to guide the actions of German commanders in combat with regard to (a) hostile military forces, (b) non-belligerents in hostile territory, and (c) neutral countries. It was phrased as the rules of the armed conflict among "civilized nations." Its prose evokes the image of the European Victorian gentleman, with much emphasis on notions of what was fair play in war and what was not.

Professor Morgan translated this edition in 1915. He prefaced it with a lengthy introduction vilifying Germans and mocking the German *War Book* as a cynical interpretation of the international laws of land warfare. Morgan's introduction is blatant propaganda and is not included here; however, his critical footnotes in the text are provided as in the original. British Prime Minister Asquith concurrently appointed a commission—known as the Boyce Commission—to investigate alleged German outrages against the civilians in neutral Belgium in the early months of the war (1914). The Boyce Commission also reviewed the German *War Book*, concluded that the Germans had violated the law of war, and used quotations from its text as another plank in the allies' wartime propaganda campaign.

The *War Book* gives the German commander guidance, as the table of contents shows, in three areas of military operations: customs of war with regard to the enemy military forces, customs of war relative to the enemy's territory and its inhabitants, and relative to the armed forces and civilian populations of neutral countries. It covered a wide variety of battlefield situations in each of the three areas of consideration.

Codification of the Law of War on Land[*]

Europeans have tried to "humanize" warfare for centuries. St. Augustine, Bishop of Hippo in the fourth century, wrote about controlling barbarism in warfare. The pope established the "Peace of God" in the eleventh century. It was not until the nineteenth century that actual international agreements to humanize warfare were made.

The first attempt to lay down specific humanitarian rules to be applicable in time of war was the so-called *Lieber Code*, drafted by Professor Francis Lieber and, after revision by a board of officers, promulgated as General Orders No. 100 of the Union Army in 1863.[†] Section II of that code, containing articles 31 to 47, provided for the "Protection of persons and especially of women, of

---

[*]Howard S. Levie, "History of the Law of War on Land," *International Review of the Red Cross*, No. 838, June 30, 2000, 339–50.

[†]*The 1863 Laws of War.* Mechanicsburg, PA: Stackpole Books, 2005. Contains the text of the Lieber Code. [Ed.]

religion, the arts and sciences," as well as "punishment of crimes against the inhabitants of hostile countries." There were also provisions requiring the humane treatment of prisoners of war. This code was a national action, but it was quickly adopted by most of the European countries.

That same year, 1863, an international conference meeting in Geneva drafted resolutions which called for each country to establish a committee to assist the medical services, and to provide for the neutrality of ambulances and medical personnel. This was the precursor for the Geneva Conferences which drafted the 1864 *Convention for the Amelioration of the Condition of the Wounded in Armies in the Field* and the 1868 *Additional Articles Relating to the Condition of the Wounded in War.*

In 1874 an international conference called by the Russian government met in Brussels and adopted the *International Declaration Concerning the Laws and Customs of War,* a document which contained many provisions intended to make land warfare more humane. Unfortunately, it never became effective for lack of ratifications. However, it served as one of the sources for the Regulations attached to the 1899 *Convention with Respect to the Laws and Customs of War on Land,* drafted by the International Peace Conference in The Hague. It was in the preamble to this conven-

tion that the famous *de Martens Clause* made its
appearance. It states:

> Until a more complete code of the laws of
> war is issued, the High Contracting Parties
> think it right to declare that in cases not
> included in the regulations adopted by them,
> populations and belligerents remain under the
> protection and empire of the principles of inter-
> national law, as they result from usages estab-
> lished between civilized nations, from the laws
> of humanity, and the requirements of the public
> conscience.

The Second International Peace Conference,
held in The Hague in 1907, adopted a slightly
redrafted set of the 1899 Regulations attached to
the *Convention Respecting the Laws and Customs
of War on Land*, which became known as the 1907
Hague Convention.

In 1906, an international conference met in
Geneva and updated the 1864 *Convention* and the
1868 *Additional Articles*. It was the 1906 *Convention for the Amelioration of the Condition of the
Wounded and Sick in Armies in the Field*, and the
1907 Hague *Convention Respecting the Laws and
Customs of War on Land* that were in force when
World War I began in 1914. Germany was a signa-
tory to these conventions, but the 1902 edition of

the *War Book* contained only the provisions of the earlier 1860s Geneva and 1899 Hague conventions. The book was not modified or supplanted either before or during World War I. As the German General Staff authors note in the introduction to the 1902 *War Book*:

> All these attempts . . . to develop, to extend, and thus to make universally binding these pre-existing usages of war; to elevate them to the level of laws binding nations and armies, in other words to create a *codex belli*—a law of war have hitherto, with some few exceptions . . . completely failed. If, therefore, in the following work the expression "the law of war" is used, it must be understood that by it is meant not a *lex scripta* [written law] introduced by international agreements, but only a *reciprocity of mutual agreement*, a limitation of arbitrary behavior, which custom and conventionality, human friendliness, and a calculating egotism have erected, *but for the observance of which there exists no express sanction, but only "the fear of reprisals."* [Emphasis added.]

Noble Precepts, Some Cynicism

There is more than a little cynicism in the General Staff's articulation of some of the customs of land warfare. Read carefully the footnotes, both those given by the General Staff authors—especially those referring to the barbarism of the French army during the Franco-Prussian War—and those provided by Professor Morgan as translator and commentator on the text. In the *War Book*, the German authors caution against "flabby emotionalism" when engaging armed enemies in uniform and out of uniform. Remember also, that Carl von Clausewitz was the elder statesman of German strategic thought. Clausewitz's dictum that "war is but an extension of politics" dominated German military thinking prior to World War I.

Another recurring theme that influenced the General Staff in this book was the behavior of the Prussian and French armies in the Franco-Prussian War of 1870–71, which was the last war both countries had fought. Memories of the events of that war were still fresh in the German General Staff's mind when the *War Book* was written in 1902.

In prosecuting wars, including the First World War, the German army was for the most part noble and honorable in the treatment of its uniformed enemies. Its treatment of civilians, politicians, and non-belligerents was less so.

While there is much to be admired in the rules of conduct contained in this book, there was much that was criticized by Germany's enemies. For instance, the officer is reminded that the civil population is to be left undisturbed in mind, body, and estate; their honor is to be inviolate; their lives are to be protected; and their property to remain secure. To compel civilians to assist the enemy is brutal, to make them betray their own country is inhuman. Such is the guidance given. Yet, a little while later the *War Book* takes a more pragmatic approach. Can an officer compel the peaceful inhabitants to give information about the strength and disposition of his country's forces? Yes, answers the *War Book*; it is doubtless regrettable, but it is often necessary. Should civilians be exposed to fire of their own troops? Yes; it may be indefensible, but its main justification is that it is successful. Should forced labor of an occupied population be limited to works which are not designed to injure their own country? No, this is an absurd distinction and impossible. Should prisoners of war be put to death? This is always ugly, but it is sometimes necessary. May one hire an assassin, or corrupt a citizen, or incite an incendiary? Certainly; it may not be reputable, and honor may militate against it, but the law of war is less touchy (explicit) on this point. Should women and children—and the old and feeble—be allowed to depart before a bombardment begins? On the contrary; their presence is greatly to be desired; it makes the bombardment all the more effective.

In the section on cunning and deceit, the German officer is instructed that there is nothing in international law against exploiting the crimes of third persons, such as assassination, incendiarism, robbery, and the like, to the disadvantage of the enemy. The British comment: "There are many things upon which international law is silent for the simple reason that it refuses to contemplate their possibility." The British of 1915 had a somewhat dated view of what was to become twentieth-century warfare, at least among the civilized nations of the world.

Terrorism and Total War
One of the most contentious points of the *War Book* is the notion of the totality of war. Many theorists would have preferred it if the laws of war were limited solely to actions relative to the enemy's army and that the laws of war were such that they eliminated altogether the possibility of military action against civilian non-belligerents. The German view was just the opposite. Field Marshal Helmut von Moltke of the German General Staff argues in one of the footnotes, "On the contrary, all the resources of the enemy, country, finances, railways, means of subsistence, even the prestige of the enemy's government ought to be attacked." British propaganda called this terrorism, that is, warfare to terrorize the civil population and its agencies. The *War Book* says, "We must seek just as hard to smash the total intellec-

tual and material resources of the enemy." Professor Morgan condemns this in his notes in the text, but by 1917 and again forty years later, in World War II, the concept of total war was wholeheartedly adopted by Great Britain and her allies.

In summary, this is an important book from many perspectives. Part I dealing with rules of warfare against one's enemy armed forces is truly honorable, noble, and chivalric—almost gentlemanly. It reflects the *noblesse oblige* of the German officer corps, which was made up primarily of nobles great and minor. Part I retains some of the chivalry of the days of old; and for the most part, the German officer did treat his soldier enemy with considerable dignity and respect.

In part II, rules for treatment of civilians and non-belligerents betray a certain nostalgia for the good old days of rape, pillage, and plunder, and a sort of grudging acceptance that Germany (the newest of the European empires) was now one of the civilized nations of the world and had to behave itself in war as a matter of national honor. On the other hand, Germany regarded many of the international laws of war to be not as pragmatic as Germany thought they needed to be in light of its then-unique views of total war. Nonetheless, this book gives the German high command's guidance that was in effect in 1914, and that guidance explains much about the Imperial German Army's behavior on the battlefields of World War I. It gives considerable insight into German thought about the nature of warfare, and it forms a context for much of what occurred in that conflict and the one that followed it twenty years later.

WAR BOOK OF THE
GERMAN GENERAL STAFF

INTRODUCTION

THE armies of belligerent States on the outbreak of
hostilities, or indeed the moment war is declared,
enter into a certain relation with one another
which is known by the name of "A State of War."
This relationship, which at the beginning only concerns the members of the two armies, is extended,
the moment the frontier is crossed, to all inhabitants of the enemy's State, so far as its territory is
occupied; indeed it extends itself ultimately to
both the movable and immovable property of the
State and its citizens.

What is a
State of
War.

A distinction is drawn between an "active" and a
"passive" state of war. By the first is to be understood the relation to one another of the actual fighting organs of the two belligerents, that is to say, of
the persons forming the army, besides that of the
representative heads of the State and of the leaders.
By the second term, *i.e.*, the "passive" state of war,
on the other hand, is to be understood the relationship of the hostile army to those inhabitants of the
State, who share in the actual conduct of war only
in consequence of their natural association with the

Active
Persons
and
Passive.

army of their own State, and who on that account are only to be regarded as enemies in a passive sense. As occupying an intermediate position, one has often to take into account a number of persons who while belonging to the army do not actually participate in the conduct of hostilities but continue in the field to pursue what is to some extent a peaceful occupation, such as Army Chaplains, Doctors, Medical Officers of Health, Hospital Nurses, Voluntary Nurses, and other Officials, Sutlers, Contractors, Newspaper Correspondents and the like.

That War is no Respecter of Persons.
Now although according to the modern conception of war, it is primarily concerned with the persons belonging to the opposing armies, yet no citizen or inhabitant of a State occupied by a hostile army can altogether escape the burdens, restrictions, sacrifices, and inconveniences which are the natural consequence of a State of War. A war conducted with energy cannot be directed merely against the combatants of the Enemy State and the positions they occupy, but it will and must in like manner seek to destroy the total intellectual[1] and material resources of the latter.[2] Humanitarian claims such as the protection of men and their goods can only be taken into consideration in so far as the nature and object of the war permit.

---

[1] [The word used is "geistig," as to the exact meaning of which see translator's footnote to page 72. What the passage amounts to is that the belligerent should seek to break the spirit of the civil population, terrorize them, humiliate them, and reduce them to despair.—J. H. M.]

[2] Moltke, in his well-known correspondence with Professor Bluntschli, is moved to denounce the St. Petersburg Convention which designs as "le seul

Consequently the "argument of war" permits The Usages of war.
every belligerent State to have recourse to all
means which enable it to attain the object of the
war; still, practise has taught the advisability of
allowing in one's own interest the introduction of a
limitation in the use of certain methods of war and
a total renunciation of the use of others. Chivalrous feelings, Christian thought, higher civilization
and, by no means least of all, the recognition of
one's own advantage, have led to a voluntary and
self-imposed limitation, the necessity of which is
to-day tacitly recognized by all States and their
armies. They have led in the course of time, in the
simple transmission of knightly usage in the pas-
sages of arms, to a series of agreements, hallowed
by tradition, and we are accustomed to sum these
up in the words "usage of war" (*Kriegsbrauch*),
"custom of war" (*Kriegssitte*), "or fashion of war"
(*Kriegsmanier*). Customs of this kind have always
existed, even in the times of antiquity; they dif-
fered according to the civilization of the different
nations and their public economy, they were not
always identical, even in one and the same conflict, and they have in the course of time often
changed; they are older than any scientific law of
war, they have come down to us unwritten, and

---

but légitime" of waging war, "l'affaiblissement des forces militaires," and this
he denies most energetically on the ground that, on the contrary, all the resources of the enemy, country, finances, railways, means of subsistence, even
the prestige of the enemy's government, ought to be attacked. [This, of course,
means the policy of "Terrorismus," *i.e.*, terrorization.—J. H. M.]

moreover they maintain themselves in full vitality; they have therefore won an assured position in standing armies according as these latter have been introduced into the systems of almost every European State.

Of the futility of Written Agreements as Scraps of Paper.   The fact that such limitations of the unrestricted and reckless application of all the available means for the conduct of war, and thereby the humanization of the customary methods of pursuing war really exist, and are actually observed by the armies of all civilized States, has in the course of the nineteenth century often led to attempts to develop, to extend, and thus to make universally binding these preexisting usages of war; to elevate them to the level of laws binding nations and armies, in other words to create a *codex belli*; a law of war. All these attempts have hitherto, with some few exceptions to be mentioned later, completely failed. If, therefore, in the following work the expression "the law of war" is used, it must be understood that by it is meant not a *lex scripta* introduced by international agreements; but only a reciprocity of mutual agreement; a limitation of arbitrary behavior, which custom and conventionality, human friendliness and a calculating egotism have erected, but for the observance of which there exists no express sanction, but only "the fear of reprisals" decides.

Consequently the usage of war is even now the only means of regulating the relations of belligerent States to one another. But with the idea of the usages of war will always be bound up the character of something transitory, inconstant, something dependent on factors outside the army. Nowadays it is not only the army which influences the spirit of the customs of war and assures recognition of its unwritten laws. Since the almost universal introduction of conscription, the peoples themselves exercise a profound influence upon this spirit. In the modern usages of war one can no longer regard merely the traditional inheritance of the ancient etiquette of the profession of arms, and the professional outlook accompanying it, but there is also the deposit of the currents of thought which agitate our time. But since the tendency of thought of the last century was dominated essentially by humanitarian considerations which not infrequently degenerated into sentimentality and flabby emotion (*Sentimentalität und weichlicher Gefühlschwarmerei*) there have not been wanting attempts to influence the development of the usages of war in a way which was in fundamental contradiction with the nature of war and its object. Attempts of this kind will also not be wanting in the future, the more so as these agitations have found a kind of moral recognition in some provisions of the Geneva Convention and the Brussels and Hague Conferences.

The "flabby emotion" of Humanitarianism.

Cruelty is
often "the
truest hu-
manity."
The perfect
Officer.

Moreover the officer is a child of his time. He is subject to the intellectual[3] tendencies which influence his own nation; the more educated he is the more will this be the case. The danger that, in this way, he will arrive at false views about the essential character of war must not be lost sight of. The danger can only be met by a thorough study of war itself. By steeping himself in military history an officer will be able to guard himself against excessive humanitarian notions, it will teach him that certain severities are indispensable to war, nay more, that the only true humanity very often lies in a ruthless application of them. It will also teach him how the rules of belligerent intercourse in war have developed, how in the course of time they have solidified into general usages of war, and finally it will teach him whether the governing usages of war are justified or not, whether they are to be modified or whether they are to be observed. But for a study of military history in this light, knowledge of the fundamental conceptions of modern international and military movements is certainly necessary. To present this is the main purpose of the following work.

---

[3] ["Den geistigen Strömungen." "Intellectual" is the nearest equivalent in English, but it barely conveys the spiritual aureole surrounding the word.— J. H. M.]

PART I

THE USAGES OF WAR IN REGARD TO THE HOSTILE ARMY

CHAPTER I

WHO BELONGS TO THE HOSTILE ARMY?

SINCE the subjects of enemy States have quite different rights and duties according as they occupy an active or a passive position, the question arises: Who is to be recognized as occupying the active position, or what amounts to the same thing—Who belongs to the hostile army? This is a question of particular importance.

According to the universal usages of war, the following are to be regarded as occupying an active position:

1. The heads of the enemy's state and its ministers, even though they possess no military rank.
2. The regular army, and it is a matter of indifference whether the army is recruited voluntarily or by conscription; whether the army consists of subjects or aliens (mercenaries); whether it is brought together out of elements which

Who are Combatants and who are not.

7

were already in the service in time of peace,
or out of such as are enrolled at the moment
of mobilization (militia, reserve, national guard
and *Landsturm*).

3. Subject to certain assumptions, irregular combatants, also, *i.e.*, such as are not constituent
parts of the regular army, but have only taken
up arms for the length of the war, or, indeed,
for a particular task of the war.

The
Irregular.

Only the third class of persons need be more
closely considered. In their case the question how
far the rights of an active position are to be conceded to them has at all times been matter of
controversy, and the treatment of irregular troops
has in consequence varied considerably. Generally
speaking the study of military history leads to the
conclusion that the Commanding Officers of regular armies were always inclined to regard irregular
troops of the enemy with distrust, and to apply to
them the contemporary laws of war with peculiar
severity. This unfavorable prejudice is based on the
ground that the want of a military education and of
stern discipline among irregular troops, easily leads
to transgressions and to non-observance of the
usages of war, and that the minor skirmishes which
they prefer to indulge in, and which by their very
nature lead to individual enterprise, open the door
to irregularity and savagery, and easily deteriorate

into robbery and unauthorized violence, so that in every case the general insecurity which it develops engenders bitterness, fury, and revengeful feelings in the harassed troops, and leads to cruel reprisals. Let any one read the combats of the French troops in the Spanish Peninsula in the years 1808 to 1814, in Tyrol in 1809, in Germany in 1813, and also those of the English in their different Colonial wars, or again the Carlist Wars, the Russo-Turkish War, and the Franco-Prussian War,[1] and one will everywhere find this experience confirmed.

If these points of view are on the whole decisive against the employment of irregular troops, yet on the other hand, it must be left to each particular State to determine how far it will disregard such considerations; from the point of view of international law no State is compelled to limit the instruments of its military operations to the standing army. It is, on the contrary, completely justified in drawing upon all the inhabitants capable of bearing arms, entirely according to its discretion, and in imparting to them an authorization to participate in the war.

Each State must decide for itself.

This public authorization has therefore been until quite recently regarded as the presumed necessary condition of any recognition of combatant rights.

The necessity of Authorization.

---

[1] [The General Staff always refers to the war of 1870 as "the German-French War."—J. H. M.]

Exceptions which prove the rule.

Of course there are numerous examples in military history in which irregular combatants have been recognized as combatants by the enemy, without any public authorization of the kind; thus in the latest wars of North America, Switzerland, and Italy, and also in the case of the campaign (without any kind of commission from a State) of Garibaldi against Naples and Sicily in the year 1860. But in all these cases the tacitly conceded recognition originated not out of any obligatory principles of international law or of military usage, but simply and solely out of the fear of reprisals. The power to prevent the entrance on the scene of these irregular partizans did not exist, and it was feared that by not recognizing their quality as combatants the war a cruel character might be given, and consequently that more harm than good might result to the parties themselves. On the other hand there

The Free Lance.

has always been a universal consensus of opinion against recognizing irregulars who make their appearance individually or in small bands, and who conduct war in some measure on their own account (*auf eigene Faust*) detached from the army, and such opinion approves of the punishment of these offenders with death.

This legal attitude which denies every unauthorized rising and identifies it with brigandage was taken up by the revolutionary armies of France towards the insurrection in La Vendée, and again by Napoleon in his proceedings against Schill and Dörnberg in the year 1809, and again by Wellington, Schwarzenberg, and Blücher, in the Proclamations issued by them in France in the year 1814, and the German Army adopted the same standpoint in the year 1870–71, when it demanded that: "Every prisoner who wishes to be treated as a prisoner of war must produce a certificate as to his character as a French soldier, issued by the legal authorities, and addressed to him personally, to the effect that he has been called to the Colors and is borne on the Roll of a corps organized on a military footing by the French Government."

In the controversies which have arisen since the war of 1870–71 over the different questions of international law and the laws of war, decisive emphasis has no longer been placed upon the question of public authorization, and it has been proposed, on grounds of expediency, to recognize as combatants such irregulars as are indeed without an express and immediate public authorization, but who are organized in military fashion and are under a responsible leader. The view here taken was that by a recognition of these kind of irregular troops the dangers and horrors of war would be diminished, and that a substitute for the legal authorization lacking in the case of individuals offers itself in the military organization and in the existence of a leader responsible to his own State.

Modern views.

Moreover the Brussels Declaration of August 27, 1874, and in consonance with it the *Manual of the Institute of International Law*, desire as the first condition of recognition as combatants "that they have at their head a personality who is responsible for the behavior of those under him to his own Government."[2]

The German Military View.

Considered from the military point of view there is not much objection to the omission of the demand for public authorization, so soon as it becomes a question of organized detachments of troops, but in the case of hostile individuals who appear on the scene we shall none the less be unable to dispense with the certificate of membership of an organized band, if such individuals are to be regarded and treated as lawful belligerents.

But the organization of irregulars in military bands and their subjection to a responsible leader are not by themselves sufficient to enable one to grant them the status of belligerents; even more important than these is the necessity of being able to recognize them as such and of their carrying their arms openly. The soldier must know who he has against him as an active opponent, he must be protected against treacherous killing and against any military operation which is prohibited by the usages of war among regular armies. The chival-

---

[2] Art. 9 (1).

rous idea which rules in the regular armies of all civilized States always seeks an open profession of one's belligerent character. The demand must, therefore, be insisted on that irregular troops, although not in uniform, shall at least be distinguishable by visible signs which are recognizable at a distance.[3] Only by such means can the occurrence of misuse in the practise of war on the one side, and the tragic consequences of the non-recognition of combatant status on the other, be made impossible. The Brussels Declarations also therefore recommend, in Art. 9 (2 and 3), that they, *i.e.*, the irregular troops, should wear a fixed sign which is visible from a distance, and that they should carry their weapons openly. The Hague Convention adds to these three conditions yet a fourth, "That they observe the laws and usages of war in their military operations."

This condition must also be maintained if it becomes a question of the *levée en masse*, the arming of the whole population of the country, province, or district; in other words the so-called

The Levée en masse.

---

[3] The necessity of an adequate mark of distinction was not denied even on the part of the French in the violent controversy which blazed up between the German and French Governments on the subject of the Franctireurs in the war of 1870-1. The dispute was mainly concerned with the question whether the marks worn by the Franctireurs were sufficient or not. This was denied on the German side in many cases with all the greater justification as the usual dress of the Franctireurs, the national blue, was not to be distinguished from the customary national dress, as it was merely a blouse furnished with a red armlet. Besides which, on the approach of German troops, the armlet was often taken off and the weapons were concealed, thereby offending against the principle of open bearing. These kind of offenses, as also the lack of a firm organization and the consequent irregularities, were the simple reason why stern treatment of the Franctireurs in the Franco-Prussian War was practised and had necessarily to be practised.

people's war or national war.[4] Starting from the view that one can never deny to the population of a country the natural right of defense of one's fatherland, and that the smaller and consequently less powerful States can only find protection in such *levées en masse*, the majority of authorities on International law have, in their proposals for codification, sought to attain the recognition on principle of the combatant status of all these kinds of people's champions, and in the Brussels declaration and the Hague Regulations the aforesaid condition[5] is omitted. As against this one may nevertheless remark that the condition requiring a military organization and a clearly recognizable mark of being attached to the enemy's troops, is not synonymous with a denial of the natural right of defense of one's country. It is therefore not a question of restraining the population from seizing arms but only of compelling it to do this in an

The Hague Regulations will not do.

organized manner. Subjection to a responsible leader, a military organization, and clear recognizability cannot be left out of account unless the whole recognized foundation for the admission of irregulars is going to be given up altogether, and a conflict of one private individual against another is

---

[4] The effacement of the distinction between fighting forces and peaceful population on the part of the Boers no doubt made many of the severities practised by the English necessary.

[5] [*i.e.*, the condition as to having a distinctive mark. So too, the Hague Regulations dispense with the other condition (of having a responsible leader and an organization) in such a case of a *levée en masse*. See Regulations, Art. II.— J. H. M.]

to be introduced again, with all its attendant horrors, of which, for example, the proceedings in Bazeilles in the last Franco-Prussian War afford an instance. If the necessary organization does not really become established—a case which is by no means likely to occur often—then nothing remains but a conflict of individuals, and those who conduct it cannot claim the rights of an active military status. The disadvantages and severities inherent in such a state of affairs are more insignificant and less inhuman than those which would result from recognition.[6]

A short way with the Defender of his Country.

---

[6] Professor Dr. C. Lüder, *Das Landkriegsrecht*, Hamburg, 1888. [This is the amiable professor who writes in Holtzendorff's *Handbach des Völkerrechts* (IV, 378) of "the terrorism so often necessary in war."—J. H. M.]

[The above paragraph, it will be observed, completely throws over Article II of the Hague Regulations extending protection to the defenders of their country.—J. H. M.]

CHAPTER II

THE MEANS OF CONDUCTING WAR

Violence and Cunning.

By the means of conducting war is to be understood all those measures which can be taken by one State against the other in order to attain the object of the war, to compel one's opponent to submit to one's will; they may be summarized in the two ideas of Violence and Cunning, and judgment as to their applicability may be embodied in the following proposition:

What is permissible includes every means of war without which the object of the war cannot be obtained; what is reprehensible on the other hand includes every act of violence and destruction which is not demanded by the object of war.

It follows from these universally valid principles that wide limits are set to the subjective freedom and arbitrary judgment of the Commanding Officer; the precepts of civilization, freedom and honor, the traditions prevalent in the army, and the general usages of war, will have to guide his decisions.

A.—MEANS OF WAR DEPENDING ON FORCE

The most important instruments of war in the possession of the enemy are his army, and his military positions; to make an end of them is the first object of war. This can happen:

1. By the annihilation, slaughter, or wounding of the individual combatants.
2. By making prisoners of the same.
3. By siege and bombardment.

1. *Annihilation, slaughter, and wounding of the hostile combatants*

In the matter of making an end of the enemy's forces by violence it is an incontestable and self-evident rule that the right of killing and annihilation in regard to the hostile combatants is inherent in the war power and its organs, that all means which modern inventions afford, including the fullest, most dangerous, and most massive means of destruction, may be utilized; these last, just because they attain the object of war as quickly as possible, are on that account to be regarded as indispensable and, when closely considered, the most human.

As a supplement to this rule, the usages of war recognize the desirability of not employing severer forms of violence if and when the object of the war may be attained by milder means, and furthermore

How to make an end of the Enemy.

The Rules of the Game.

that certain means of war which lead to unnecessary suffering are to be excluded. To such belong:

The use of poison both individually and collectively (such as poisoning of streams and food supplies[1]) the propagation of infectious diseases.

Assassination, proscription, and outlawry of an opponent.[2]

The use of arms which cause useless suffering, such as soft-nosed bullets, glass, etc.

The killing of wounded or prisoners who are no longer capable of offering resistance.[3]

The refusal of quarter to soldiers who have laid down their arms and allowed themselves to be captured.

The progress of modern invention has made superfluous the express prohibition of certain old-fashioned but formerly legitimate instruments of war (chain shot, red-hot shot, pitch balls, etc.), since others, more effective, have been substituted for these; on the other hand the use of projectiles of less than 400 grammes in weight is prohibited by

[1] Notoriously resorted to very often in the war of the Spanish against Napoleon.

[2] Napoleon was, in the year 1815, declared an outlaw by the Allies. Such a proceeding is not permissible by the International Law of to-day since it involves an indirect invitation to assassination. Also the offer of a reward for the capture of a hostile prince or commander as occurred in August, 1813, on the part of the Crown Prince of Sweden in regard to Napoleon, is no longer in harmony with the views of today and the usages of war. [But to hire a third person to assassinate one's opponent is claimed by the German General Staff (see II, b, below) as quite legitimate.—J. H. M]

[3] As against this there have been many such offenses committed in the wars of recent times, principally on the Turkish side in the Russo-Turkish War.

the St. Petersburg Convention of December 11th, 1868. (This only in the case of musketry.[4])

He who offends against any of these prohibitions is to be held responsible therefore by the State. If he is captured he is subject to the penalties of military law.

Closely connected with the unlawful instruments of war is the employment of uncivilized and barbarous peoples in European wars. Looked at from the point of view of law it can, of course, not be forbidden to any State to call up armed forces from its extra-European colonies, but the practise stands in express contradiction to the modern movement for humanizing the conduct of war and for alleviating its attendant sufferings, if men and troops are employed in war, who are without the knowledge of civilized warfare and by whom, therefore, the very cruelties and inhumanities forbidden by the usages of war are committed. The employment of these kinds of troops is therefore to be compared with the use of the instruments of war already described as forbidden. The transplantation of African and Mohammedan Turcos to a European seat of war in the year 1870 was, therefore, undoubtedly to be regarded as a retrogression from civilized to barbarous warfare, since these troops had and could have no conception of

Colored Troops are "Blacklegs."

---

[4] This prohibition was often sinned against by the French in the war of 1870–71. Cp. Bismarck's despatches of Jan. 9th and Feb. 7th, 1871; also Bluntschli in *Holtzendorf's Jahrbuch*, I, p. 279, where a similar reproach brought against the Baden troops is refuted.

European-Christian culture, or respect for property and for the honor of women, etc.[5]

2. *Capture of Enemy Combatants*

Prisoners
of War.

If individual members or parties of the army fall into the power of the enemy's forces, either through their being disarmed and defenseless, or through their being obliged to cease from hostilities in consequence of a formal capitulation, they are then in the position of "prisoners of war," and thereby in some measure exchange an active for a passive position.

Vae Victis!

According to the older doctrine of international law all persons belonging to the hostile State, whether combatants or non-combatants, who happen to fall into the hands of their opponent, are in the position of prisoners of war. He could deal with them according to his pleasure, ill-treat them, kill them, lead them away into bondage, or sell them into slavery. History knows but few exceptions to this rule, these being the result of particular treaties. In the Middle Ages the Church tried to intervene as mediator in order to ameliorate the lot

---

[5] If we have principally in view the employment of uncivilized and barbarous troops on a European seat of war, that is simply because the war of 1870 lies nearest to us in point of time and of space. On a level with it is the employment of Russo-Asiatic nationalities in the wars of emancipation, of Indians in the North-American War, of the Circassians in the Polish Rising, of the Bashi-bazouks in the Russo-Turkish War, etc. As regards the Turcos, a Belgian writer Rolin-Jacquémyns said of them in regard to the war of 1859, "les allures et le conduite des Turcos avaient soulevé d'universels dégoûts." On the other side it is not to be forgotten that a section of the French Press in 1870 praised them precisely because of their bestialities and incited them to such things, thus in the *Independence algerienne*: "Arrière la pitié! arrière les sentiments d'human-ité! Mort, pillage et incendie!"

of the prisoners, but without success. Only the prospect of ransom, and chivalrous ideas in the case of individuals, availed to give any greater protection. It is to be borne in mind that the prisoners belonged to him who had captured them, a conception which began to disappear after the Thirty Years' War. The treatment of prisoners of war was mostly harsh and inhuman; still, in the seventeenth century, it was usual to secure their lot by a treaty on the outbreak of a war.

The credit of having opened the way to another conception of war captivity belongs to Frederick the Great and Franklin, inasmuch as they inserted in the famous Treaty of friendship, concluded in 1785 between Prussia and North America, entirely new regulations as to the treatment of prisoners of war.

The complete change in the conception of war *The Modern View.* introduced in recent times has in consequence changed all earlier ideas as to the position and treatment of prisoners of war. Starting from the principle that only States and not private persons are in the position of enemies in time of war, and that an enemy who is disarmed and taken prisoner is no longer an object of attack, the doctrine of war captivity is entirely altered and the position of prisoners has become assimilated to that of the wounded and the sick.

The present position of international law and *Prisoners of War are to be honorably treated.* the law of war on the subject of prisoners of war is based on the fundamental conception that they are the captives not of private individuals, that is to say of Commanders, Soldiers, or Detachments of Troops, but that they are the captives of the State. But the State regards them as persons who have simply done their duty and obeyed the commands of their superiors, and in consequence views their captivity not as penal but merely as precautionary.

It therefore follows that the object of war captivity is simply to prevent the captives from taking any further part in the war, and that the State can, in fact, do everything which appears necessary for securing the captives, but nothing beyond that. The captives have therefore to submit to all those restrictions and inconveniences which the purpose of securing them necessitates; they can collectively be involved in a common suffering if some individuals among them have provoked sterner treatment; but, on the other hand, they are protected against unjustifiable severities, ill-treatment, and unworthy handling; they do, indeed, lose their freedom, but not their rights; war captivity is, in other words, no longer an act of grace on the part of the victor but a right of the defenseless.

Who may be made Prisoners.   According to the notions of the laws of war today the following persons are to be treated as prisoners of war:

1. The Sovereign, together with those members of his family who were capable of bearing arms, the chief of the enemy's State, generally speaking, and the Ministers who conduct its policy even though they are not among the individuals belonging to the active army.[6]

2. All persons belonging to the armed forces.

3. All Diplomatists and Civil Servants attached to the army.

4. All civilians staying with the army, with the approval of its Commanders, such as transport, sutlers, contractors, newspaper correspondents, and the like.

5. All persons actively concerned with the war such as Higher Officials, Diplomatists, Couriers, and the like, as also all those persons whose freedom can be a danger to the army of the other State, for example, Journalists of hostile opinions, prominent and influential leaders of Parties, Clergy who excite the people, and such like.[7]

6. The mass of the population of a province or a district if they rise in defense of their country.

---

[6] Recent examples: the capture of the King of Saxony by the Allies after the Battle of Leipzig, and also of Napoleon, that of the Elector of Hesse, 1866, Napoleon III, 1870, Abdel-Kader, 1847, and Schamyl, 1859.

[7] In this light must be judged the measures taken in 1866 by General Vogel von Falckenstein against certain Hanoverian citizens although these measures have often been represented in another light.

The points of view regarding the treatment of prisoners of war may be summarized in the following rules:

Prisoners of war are subject to the laws of the State which has captured them.

The treat-
ment of
Prisoners
of War.

The relation of the prisoners of war to their own former superiors ceases during their captivity; a captured officer's servant steps into the position of a private servant. Captured officers are never the superiors of soldiers of the State which has captured them; on the contrary, they are under the orders of such of the latter as are entrusted with their custody.

The prisoners of war have, in the places in which they are quartered, to submit to such restrictions of their liberty as are necessary for their safe keeping. They have strictly to comply with the obligation imposed upon them, not to move beyond a certain indicated boundary.

Their con-
finement.

These measures for their safe keeping are not to be exceeded; in particular, penal confinement, fetters, and unnecessary restrictions of freedom are only to be resorted to if particular reasons exist to justify or necessitate them.

The concentration camps in which prisoners of war are quartered must be as healthy, clean, and decent as possible; they should not be prisons or convict establishments.

It is true that the French captives were transported by the Russians to Siberia as malefactors in the years 1812 and 1813. This was a measure which was not illegitimate according to the older practise of war, but it is no longer in accordance with the legal conscience of to-day. Similarly the methods which were adopted during the Civil War in North America in a prison in the Southern States, against prisoners of war of the Union Forces, whereby the men were kept without air and nourishment and thus badly treated, were also against the practise of the law of war.

Freedom of movement within these concentration camps or within the whole locality may be permitted if there are no special reasons against it. But obviously prisoners of war are subject to the existing, or to the appointed rules of the establishment or garrison.

Prisoners of war can be put to moderate work proportionate to their position in life; work is a safeguard against excesses. Also on grounds of health this is desirable. But these tasks should not be prejudicial to health nor in any way dishonorable or such as contribute directly or indirectly to the military operations against the Fatherland of the captives. Work for the State is, according to the Hague regulations, to be paid at the rates payable to members of the army of the State itself.

The Prisoner and his Taskmaster.

Should the work be done on account of other public authorities or of private persons, then the conditions will be fixed by agreement with the military authorities. The wages of the prisoners of war must be expended in the improvement of their condition, and anything that remains should be paid over to them after deducting the cost of their maintenance when they are set free. Voluntary work in order to earn extra wages is to be allowed, if there are no particular reasons against it.[8] Insurrection, insubordination, misuse of the freedom granted, will of course justify severer confinement in each case, also punishment, and so will crimes and misdemeanors.

Flight.   Attempts at escape on the part of individuals who have not pledged their word of honor might be regarded as the expression of a natural impulse for liberty, and not as a crime. They are therefore to be punished by restriction of the privileges granted and a sharper supervision but not with death. But the latter punishment will follow of course in the case of plots to escape, if only because of the danger of them. In case of a breach of a man's parole the punishment of death may reasonably be incurred. In some circumstances, if necessity and the behavior of the prisoners compel it, one is justified in taking measures the effect of which is to involve the innocent with the guilty.[9]

Diet.   The food of the prisoners must be sufficient and suitable to their rank, yet they will have to be

---

[8] Thus the French prisoners in 1870–1 were very thankful to find employment in great numbers as harvest workers, or in the counting houses of merchants or in the factories of operatives or wherever an opportunity occurred, and were thereby enabled to earn extra wages.

[9] Thus General von Falckenstein in 1870, in order to check the prevalent escaping of French officers, commanded that for every escape ten officers

content with the customary food of the country; luxuries which the prisoners wish to get at their own expense are to be permitted if reasons of discipline do not forbid.

Correspondence with one's home is to be permitted, likewise visits and intercourse, but these of course must be watched. *Letters.*

The prisoners of war remain in possession of their private property with the exception of arms, horses, and documents of a military purport. If for definite reasons any objects are taken away from them, then these must be kept in suitable places and restored to them at the end of their captivity. *Personal belongings.*

Article 14 of the Hague Regulations prescribes that on the outbreak of hostilities there shall be established in each of the belligerent States and in a given case in neutral States, which have received into their territory any of the combatants, an information bureau for prisoners of war. Its duty will be to answer all inquiries concerning such prisoners and to receive the necessary particulars from the services concerned in order to be able to keep a personal entry for every prisoner. The information bureau must always be kept well posted about everything which concerns a prisoner of war. Also *The Information Bureau.*

---

whose names were to be determined by drawing lots should be sent off, with the loss of all privileges of rank, to close confinement in a Prussian fortress, a measure which was, indeed, often condemned but against which nothing can be said on the score of the law of nations.

this information bureau must collect and assign to the legitimate persons all personal objects, valuables, letters, and the like, which are found on the field of battle or have been left behind by dead prisoners of war in hospitals or field-hospitals. The information bureau enjoys freedom from postage, as do generally all postal despatches sent to or by prisoners of war. Charitable gifts for prisoners of war must be free of customs duty and also of freight charges on the public railways.

The prisoners of war have, in the event of their being wounded or sick, a claim to medical assistance and care as understood by the Geneva Convention and, so far as is possible, to spiritual ministrations also.

These rules may be shortly summarized as follows:

Prisoners of war are subject to the laws of the country in which they find themselves, particularly the rules in force in the army of the local State; they are to be treated like one's own soldiers, neither worse nor better.

When Prisoners may be put to Death.

The following considerations hold good as regard the imposition of a death penalty in the case of prisoners; they can be put to death:

1. In case they commit offenses or are guilty of practises which are punishable by death by civil or military laws.

2. In case of insubordination, attempts at escape, etc., deadly weapons can be employed.

3. In case of overwhelming necessity, as reprisals, either against similar measures, or against other irregularities on the part of the management of the enemy's army.

4. In case of overwhelming necessity, when other means of precaution do not exist and the existence of the prisoners becomes a danger to one's own existence.

As regards the admissibility of reprisals, it is to be remarked that these are objected to by numerous teachers of international law on grounds of humanity. To make this a matter of principle, and apply it to every case exhibits, however, "a misconception due to intelligible but exaggerated and unjustifiable feelings of humanity, of the significance, the seriousness and the right of war. It must not be overlooked that here also the necessity of war, and the safety of the State are the first consideration, and not regard for the unconditional freedom of prisoners from molestation."[10]

"Reprisals."

That prisoners should only be killed in the event of extreme necessity, and that only the duty of self-preservation and the security of one's own State can justify a proceeding of this kind is to-day

One must not be too scrupulous.

---

[10] [Professor] Lueder, *Das Landkriegsrecht*, p. 73.

universally admitted. But that these considerations have not always been decisive is proved by the shooting of 2,000 Arabs at Jaffa in 1799 by Napoleon; of the prisoners in the rising of La Vendée; in the Carlist War; in Mexico, and in the American War of Secession, where it was generally a case of deliverance from burdensome supervision and the difficulties of maintenance; whereas peoples of a higher morality such as the Boers in our own days, finding themselves in a similar position, have preferred to let their prisoners go. For the rest, calamities such as might lead to the shooting of prisoners are scarcely likely to happen under the excellent conditions of transport in our own time and the correspondingly small difficulty of feeding them—in a European campaign.[11]

The end of Captivity.

The captivity of war comes to an end:

1. By force of circumstances which *de facto* determine it, for example, successful escape, cessation of the war, or death.
2. By becoming the subject of the enemy's state.
3. By release, whether conditional or unconditional, unilateral or reciprocal.
4. By exchange.

---

[11] What completely false notions about the right of killing prisoners of war are prevalent even among educated circles in France is shown by the widely-circulated novel *Les Braves Gens*, by Margueritte, in which, on page 360 of the chapter "Mon Premier," is told the story, based apparently on an actual occurrence, of the shooting of a captured Prussian soldier, and it is excused simply because the information given by him as to the movements of his own people turned out to be untrue. The cowardly murder of a defenseless man is

As to 1. With the cessation of the war every reason for the captivity ceases, provided there exist no special grounds for another view. It is on that account that care should be taken to discharge prisoners immediately. There remain only prisoners sentenced to punishment or awaiting trial, *i.e.*, until the expiation of their sentence or the end of their trial as the case may be.

As to 2. This pre-supposes the readiness of the State to accept the prisoner as a subject.

As to 3. A man released under certain conditions has to fulfil them without question. If he does not do this, and again falls into the hands of his enemy, then he must expect to be dealt with by military law, and indeed according to circumstances with the punishment of death. A conditional release cannot be imposed on the captive; still less is there any obligation upon the state to discharge a prisoner on conditions—for example, on his parole. The release depends entirely on the discretion of the State, as does also the determination of its limits and the persons to whom it shall apply.

Parole.

The release of whole detachments on their parole is not usual. It is rather to be regarded as an arrangement with each particular individual.

---

regarded by the author as a stern duty, due to war, and is thus declared to be in accordance with the usages of war. [The indignation of the German General Staff is somewhat overdone, as a little further on (see the chapter on treatment of inhabitants of occupied territory) in the War Book they advocate the ruthless shooting or hanging of an inhabitant who, being *forced* to guide an enemy army against his own, leads them astray.—J. H. M.]

Arrangements of this kind, every one of which
is as a rule made a conditional discharge, must be
very precisely formulated and the wording of them
most carefully scrutinized. In particular it must be
precisely expressed whether the person released is
only bound no longer to fight directly with arms
against the State which releases him, in the present
war, whether he is justified in rendering services to
his own country in other positions or in the
colonies, etc., or whether all and every kind of
service is forbidden him.

The question whether the parole given by an
officer or a soldier is recognized as binding or not
by his own State depends on whether the legislation or even the military instructions permit or forbid the giving of one's parole.[12] In the first case his
own State must not command him to do services
the performance of which he has pledged himself
not to undertake.[13] But personally the man
released on parole is under all circumstances
bound to observe it. He destroys his honor if he
breaks his word, and is liable to punishment if
recaptured, even though he has been hindered by
his own State from keeping it.[14] According to

---

[12] In Austria the giving of one's parole whether by troops or officers is forbidden.

[13] Monod, *Allemands et Français, Souvenirs de Campagne*, p. 39: "I saw
again at Tours some faces which I had met before Sedan; among them were,
alas! officers who had sworn not to take up arms again, and who were preparing to violate their parole, encouraged by a Government in whom the sense of
honor was as blunted as the sense of truth."

[14] In the year 1870, 145 French officers, including three Generals, one
Colonel, two Lieutenant-Colonels, three Commandants, thirty Captains

the Hague Regulations a Government can demand no services which are in conflict with a man's parole.

As to 4. The exchange of prisoners in a single case can take place between two belligerents without its being necessary in every case to make circumstantial agreements. As regards the scope of the exchange and the forms in which it is to be completed the Commanding Officers on both sides alone decide. Usually the exchange is man for man, in which case the different categories of military persons are taken into account and certain ratios established as to what constitutes equivalents.

Transport of Prisoners.—Since no Army makes prisoners in order to let them escape again afterwards, measures must be taken for their transport in order to prevent attempts at escape. If one recalls that in the year 1870–71, no fewer than 11,160 officers and 333,885 men were brought from France to Germany, and as a result many thousands often had to be guarded by a proportionately small company, one must admit that in such a position only the most zealous energy and ruthless employment of all the means at one's disposal can avail, and although it is opposed to military sentiment to use weapons against the defenseless, none

Exchange of Prisoners.

Removal of Prisoners.

(Bismarck's Despatch of December 14th, 1870), were guilty of breaking their parole. The excuses, afterwards put forward, were generally quite unsound, though perhaps there may have been an element of doubt in some of the cases so positively condemned on the German side. The proceedings of the French Government who allowed these persons without scruple to take service again were subsequently energetically denounced by the National Assembly.

the less in such a case one has no other choice. The captive who seeks to free himself by flight does so at his peril and can complain of no violence which the custody of prisoners directs in order to prevent behavior of that kind. Apart from these apparently harsh measures against attempt at escape, the transport authorities must do everything they can to alleviate the lot of the sick and wounded prisoners, in particular they are to protect them against insults and ill-treatment from an excited mob.

3. *Sieges and Bombardments*

Fair Game.   War is waged not merely with the hostile combatants but also with the inanimate military resources of the enemy. This includes not only the fortresses but also every town and every village which is an obstacle to military progress. All can be besieged and bombarded, stormed and destroyed, if they are defended by the enemy, and in some cases even if they are only occupied. There has always been a divergence of views, among Professors of International Law, as to the means which are permissible for waging war against these inanimate objects, and these views have frequently been in strong conflict with those of soldiers; it is therefore necessary to go into this question more closely.

We have to distinguish:

(*a*) Fortresses, strong places, and fortified places.

(*b*) Open towns, villages, buildings, and the like, which, however, are occupied or used for military purposes.

Fortresses and strong places are important centers of defense, not merely in a military sense, but also in a political and economic sense. They furnish a principal resource to the enemy and can therefore be bombarded just like the hostile army itself.

A preliminary notification of bombardment is just as little to be required as in the case of a sudden assault. The claims to the contrary put forward by some jurists are completely inconsistent with war and must be repudiated by soldiers; the cases in which a notification has been voluntarily given do not prove its necessity. The besieger will have to consider for himself the question whether the very absence of notification may not be itself a factor of success, by means of surprise, and indeed whether notification will not mean a loss of precious time. If there is no danger of this then humanity no doubt demands such a notification.

Of making the most of one's opportunity.

Since town and fortifications belong together and form an inseparable unity, and can seldom in a military sense, and never in an economic and political sense, be separated, the bombardment will not limit itself to the actual fortification, but it will and must extend over the whole town; the reason for this lies in the fact that a restriction of the bombardment to the fortifications is impracticable; it would jeopardize the success of the operation, and would quite unjustifiably protect the defenders who are not necessarily quartered in the works.

Spare the Churches.

But this does not preclude the exemption by the besieger of certain sections and buildings of the fortress or town from bombardment, such as churches, schools, libraries, museums, and the like, so far as this is possible.

But of course it is assumed that buildings seeking this protection will be distinguishable and that they are not put to defensive uses. Should this happen, then every humanitarian consideration must give way. The utterances of French writers about the bombardments of Strasburg Cathedral in the year 1870, are therefore quite without justification, since it only happened after an observatory for officers of artillery had been erected on the tower.

The only exemption from bombardment recognized by international law, through the medium of the Geneva Convention, concerns hospitals and convalescent establishments. Their extension is left to the discretion of the besieger.

A Bombardment is no Respecter of Persons.

As regards the civil population of a fortified place the rule is: All the inhabitants, whether natives or foreigners, whether permanent or temporary residents, are to be treated alike.

No exception need be made in regard to the diplomatists of neutral States who happen to be in the town; if before or during the investment by the besieger their attention is drawn to the fate to which they expose themselves by remaining, and if days of grace in which to leave are afforded them, that simply rests on the courtesy of the besieger. No such duty is incumbent upon him in international law. Also permission to send out couriers with diplomatic despatches depends entirely upon the discretion of the besieger. In any case it will always depend on whether the necessary security against misuse is provided.[15]

If the commandant of a fortress wishes to strengthen its defensive capacity by expelling a portion of the population such as women, children, old people, wounded, etc., then he must take these steps in good time, *i.e.*, before the investment begins. If the investment is completed, no claim to the free passage of these classes can be made good. All juristic demands to the contrary are as a matter of principle to be repudiated, as being in fundamental conflict with the principles of war. The very presence of such persons may accelerate

A timely severity.

---

[15] To a petition of the diplomatists shut up in Paris to be allowed to send a courier at least once a week, Bismarck answered in a document of September 27th, 1870, as follows: "The authorization of exchange of correspondence in the case of a fortress is not generally one of the usages of war; and although we would authorize willingly the forwarding of open letters from diplomatic agents, in so far as their contents be not inconvenient from a military point of view, I cannot recognize as well founded the opinion of those who should consider the interior of the fortifications of Paris as a suitable center for diplomatic relations."

the surrender of the place in certain circumstances, and it would therefore be foolish of a
besieger to renounce voluntarily this advantage.[16]

Once the surrender of a fortress is accom-
plished, then, by the usages of war to-day, any further destruction, annihilation, incendiarism, and
the like, are completely excluded. The only further
injuries that are permitted are those demanded or
necessitated by the object of the war, *e.g.*, destruction of fortifications, removal of particular buildings, or in some circumstances of complete
quarters, rectification of the foreground and so on.

"Undefend-
ed Places." A prohibition by international law of the bombardment of open towns and villages which are not
occupied by the enemy, or defended, was, indeed,
put into words by the Hague Regulations, but
appears superfluous, since modern military history
knows of hardly any such case.

But the matter is different where open towns
are occupied by the enemy or are defended. In this
case, naturally all the rules stated above as to fortified places hold good, and the simple rules of tac-
tics dictate that fire should be directed not merely
against the bounds of the place, so that the space

---

[16] "In the year 1870 the greatest mildness was practised on the German side
towards the French fortresses. At the beginning of the siege of Strassburg it
was announced to the French Commander that free passage was granted to the
women, the children, and the sick, a favor which General Uhrich rejected, and
the offer of which he very wisely did not make known to the population. And
when later three delegates of the Swiss Federal Council sought permission in
accordance with the resolution of the Conference at Olten, of September 7th,
to carry food to the civil population in Strassburg and to conduct non-combatants out of the town over the frontier, both requests were willingly granted by
the besieger and four thousand inhabitants left the fortress as a result of this-
permission. Lastly, the besiegers of Belfort granted to the women, children,

behind the enemy's firing line and any reserves that may be there shall not escape. A bombardment is indeed justified, and unconditionally dictated by military consideration, if the occupation of the village is not with a view to its defense but only for the passage of troops, or to screen an approach or retreat, or to prepare or cover a tactical movement, or to take up supplies, etc. The only criterion is the value which the place possesses for the enemy in the existing situation.

Regarding it from this point of view, the bombardment of Kehl by the French in 1870 was justified by military necessity, although the place bombarded was an open town and not directly defended. "Kehl offered the attacking force the opportunity of establishing itself in its buildings, and of bringing up and placing there its personnel and material, unseen by the defenders. It became a question of making Kehl inaccessible to the enemy and of depriving it of the characteristics which made its possession advantageous to the enemy. The aforesaid justification was not very evident."[17]

Also the bombardment of the open town of Saarbrücken cannot from the military point of

---

aged, and sick, free passage to Switzerland, not indeed immediately at the moment chosen by the commander Denfert, but indeed soon after" (*Dahn*, I, p. 89). Two days after the bombardment of Bitsch had begun (September 11th) the townsfolk begged for free passage out of the town. This was, indeed, officially refused; but, none the less, by the indulgence of the besieger, it was effected by a great number of townspeople. Something like one-half of the 2,700 souls of the civil population, including the richest and most respectable, left the town (*Irle, die Festung Bitsch. Beiträge zur Lander und Völkerkunde von Elsass-Lothringen*).

[17] Hartmann, *Krit. Versuche*, II, p. 83.

view be the subject of reproach against the French. On August 2nd a Company of the Fusilier Regiment No. 40 had actually occupied the railway station and several others had taken up a position in the town. It was against these troops that the fire of the French was primarily directed. If havoc was spread in the town, that could scarcely be avoided. In the night of August 3rd to 4th, the fire of the French batteries was again directed on the railway station in order to prevent the despatch of troops and material. Against this proceeding also no objection can be made, since the movement of trains had actually taken place.

If, therefore, on the German side[18] energetic protest were made in both cases, and the bombardment of Kehl and Saarbrücken were declared a violation of international law, this only proves that in 1870 a proper comprehension of questions of the laws of war of this kind was not always to be found even in the highest military and official circles. But still less was this the case on the French side as is clear from the protests against the German bombardment of Dijon, Chateaudun, Baz-

---

[18] *Staatsanzeiger*, August 26th, 1870.

[19] Considering the many unintelligible things written on the French side about this, the opinion of an objective critic is doubly valuable. Monod, p. 55, *op. cit.*, says: "I have seen Bazeilles burning; I have informed myself with the greatest care as to how things happened. I have questioned French soldiers, Bavarian soldiers, and Bavarian inhabitants present at this terrible drama; I am able to see in it only one of the frightful, but inevitable, consequences of the war." As to the treatment of Chateaudun, stigmatized generally on the French side as barbarous, the author writes (p. 56): "The inhabitants of Chateaudun, regularly organized as part of the National Guard, aided by the franctireurs of Paris, do not defend themselves by preparing ambushes but by fighting as soldiers. Chateaudun is bombarded; nothing could be more legitimate, since the

eilles, and other places, the military justification for which is still clearer and incontestable.[19]

B.—METHODS NOT INVOLVING THE USE OF FORCE.
CUNNING, AND DECEIT

Cunning in war has been permissible from the earliest times, and was esteemed all the more as it furthered the object of war without entailing the loss of men. Surprises, laying of ambushes, feigned attacks and retreats, feigned flight, pretense of inactivity, spreading of false news as to one's strength and dispositions, use of the enemy's parole—all this was permitted and prevalent ever since war begun, and so it is to-day.[20]

Stratagems.

As to the limits between recognized stratagems and those forms of cunning which are reprehensible, contemporary opinion, national culture, the practical needs of the moment, and the changing military situation, are so influential that it is prima facie proportionately difficult to draw any recognized limit, as difficult as between criminal selfishness and taking a justifiable advantage. Some forms of artifice are, however, under all circum-

What are "dirty tricks"?

---

inhabitants made a fortress of it; but once they got the upper hand the Bavarians set fire to more than one hundred houses." The picture of outrages by Germans which follows may be countered by what the author writes in another place about the French soldiers: "The frightful scenes at the taking of Paris by our troops at the end of May, 1871, may enable us to understand what violences soldiers allow themselves to be drawn into, when both excited and exhausted by the conflict."

[20] "One makes use in war of the skin of the lion or the fox indifferently. Cunning often succeeds where force would fail; it is therefore absolutely necessary to make use of both; sometimes force can be countered by force, while on the other hand force has often to yield to cunning."—Frederick the Great, in his *General Principles of War*, Art. xi.

The apophthegm of Frederick the Great.

stances irreconcilable with honorable fighting, especially all those which take the form of faithlessness,
fraud, and breach of one's word. Among these are
breach of a safe-conduct; of a free retirement; or of
an armistice, in order to gain by a surprise attack an
advantage over the enemy; feigned surrender in
order to kill the enemy who then approach unsuspi-
ciously; misuse of a flag of truce, or of the Red
Cross, in order to secure one's approach, or in case
of attack, deliberate violation of a solemnly concluded obligation, *e.g.*, of a war treaty; incitement to
crime, such as murder of the enemy's leaders, incendiarism, robbery, and the like. This kind of outrage
was an offense against the law of nations even in the
earliest times. The natural conscience of mankind
whose spirit is chivalrously alive in the armies of all
civilized States, has branded it as an outrage upon
human right, and enemies who in such a public manner violate the laws of honor and justice have been
regarded as no longer on an equality.[21]

The views of military authorities about methods
of this kind, as also of those which are on the bor-
derline, frequently differ from the views held by
notable jurists. So also the putting on of enemy's
uniforms, the employment of enemy or neutral
flags and marks, with the object of deception are

---

[21] Also the pretense of false facts, as, for example, practised by Murat on November 13th, 1805, against Prince Auersperg, in order to get possession of the
passage of the Danube at Florisdorf; the like stratagem which a few days later
Bagration practised against Murat at Schongraben; the deceptions under cover
of their word of honor practised by the French Generals against the Prussian
leaders in 1806 at Prenzlau; these are stratagems which an officer in the field
would scarcely dare to employ to-day without being branded by the public
opinion of Europe.

as a rule declared permissible by the theory of the laws of war,[22] while military writers[23] have expressed themselves unanimously against them. The Hague Conference has adopted the latter view in forbidding the employment of enemy's uniforms and military marks equally with the misuse of flags of truce and of the Red Cross.[24]

Of False Uniforms.

Bribery of the enemy's subjects with the object of obtaining military advantages, acceptance of offers of treachery, reception of deserters, utilization of the discontented elements in the population, support of pretenders and the like, are permissible, indeed in international law is in no way opposed[25] to the exploitation of the crimes of third parties (assassination, incendiarism, robbery, and the like) to the prejudice of the enemy.

The Corruption of others may be useful.

And murder is one of the Fine Arts.

---

[22] In the most recent times a change of opinion seems to have taken place. Bluntsehli in his time holds (sec. 565) the use of the distinguishing marks of the enemy's army—uniforms, standards, and flags—with the object of deception, to be a doubtful practise, and thinks that this kind of deception should not extend beyond the preparations for battle. "In battle the opponents should engage one another openly, and should not fall on an enemy from behind in the mask of a friend and brother in arms." The Manual of the Institute of International Law goes further. It says in 8 (c and d): "Il est interdit d'attaquer l'ennemi en dissimulant les signes distinctifs de la force armée; d'user ind'ment du pavillon national, des insignes militaires ou de l'uniforme de l'ennemi." The Declaration of Brussels altered the original proposition, "L'emploi du pavillon national ou des insignes militaires et de l'uniforme de l'ennemi est interdit" into "L'abus du pavillon national."

[23] Cp. Boguslawski, *Der kleine Krieg*, 1881, pp. 26, 27.

[24] [The Hague Regulations, Art. 23, to which Germany was a party, declares it is prohibited: "To make improper use of a flag of truce, the national flag, or military ensigns and the enemy's uniform, as well as the distinctive badges of the Geneva Convention."—J. H. M.]

[25] [This represents the German War Book in its most disagreeable light, and is casuistry of the worst kind. There are certain things on which International Law is silent because it will not admit the possibility of their existence. As Professor Holland well puts it (*The Laws of War on Land*, p. 61), in reference to the subject of reprisals the Hague Conference "declined to seem to add to the authority of a practise so repulsive" by legislating on the subject. And so with assassination. It can never be presumed from the Hague or other international agreements that what is not expressly forbidden is thereby approved.]

Considerations of chivalry, generosity, and honor may denounce in such cases a hasty and unsparing exploitation of such advantages as indecent and dishonorable, but law which is less touchy allows it.[26] "The ugly and inherently immoral aspect of such methods cannot affect the recognition of their lawfulness. The necessary aim of war gives the belligerent the right and imposes upon him, according to circumstances, the duty not to let slip the important, it may be the decisive, advantages to be gained by such means."[27]

---

[26] [Professor] Bluntsehli, *Völkerrecht*, p. 316.

[27] [Professor] Lüder, *Handbuch des Völkerrechts*, p. 90.

CHAPTER III

TREATMENT OF WOUNDED AND SICK SOLDIERS

THE generally accepted principle that in war one should do more harm to one's enemy than the object of the war unconditionally requires, has led to treating the wounded and sick combatants as being no longer enemies, but merely sick men who are to be taken care of and as much as possible protected from the tragic results of wounds and illness. Although endeavors to protect the wounded soldiers from arbitrary slaughter, mutilation, illtreatment, or other brutalities go back to the oldest times, yet the credit of systematizing these endeavors belongs to the nineteenth century, and this system was raised to the level of a principle of international law by the Geneva Convention of 1864.

With the elevation of the Geneva Agreements to the level of laws binding peoples and armies, the question of the treatment of wounded and sick combatants, as well as that of the persons devoted to the healing and care of them, is separated from the usages of war. Moreover, and discussion of the form of this international law must be regarded from the military point of view as aimless and

The sanctity of the Geneva Convention.

45

unprofitable. The soldier may still be convinced
that some of the Articles are capable of improvement, that others need supplementing, and that yet
others should be suppressed, but he has not the
right to deviate from the stipulations; it is his duty
to contribute as far as he can to the observance of
the whole code.

The
"Hyenas of
the Battle-
field."

No notice is taken in the Geneva Convention of
the question of the protection of fallen or wounded
combatants from the front, from the rabble usually
known as "The Hyenas of the battlefield," who are
accustomed to rob, ill-treat, or slay soldiers lying
defenseless on the field of battle. This is a matter left
to the initiative of the troops. Persons of this kind,
whether they be soldiers or not, are undoubtedly to
be dealt with in the sternest possible manner.

CHAPTER IV

INTERCOURSE BETWEEN BELLIGERENT ARMIES

HOSTILE armies are in frequent intercourse with one another. This takes place so long as it is practised openly, that is to say, with the permission of the commanders on both sides, by means of bearers of flags of truce. In this class are included those who have to conduct the official intercourse between the belligerent armies or divisions thereof, and who appear as authorized envoys of one army to the other, in order to conduct negotiations and to transmit communications. As to the treatment of bearers of flags of truce there exist regular usages of war, an intimate acquaintance with which is of the highest practical importance. This knowledge is not merely indispensable for the higher officers, but also for all inferior officers, and to a certain extent for the private in the ranks.

Since a certain degree of intercourse between the two belligerents is unavoidable, and indeed desirable, the assurance of this intercourse is in the interests of both parties; it has held good as a custom from the earliest times, and even among uncivilized people, whereby these envoys and their assistants (trumpeter, drummer, interpreter, and

Flags of Truce.

orderly) are to be regarded as inviolable; a custom which proceeds on the presumption that these persons, although drawn from the ranks of the combatants, are no longer, during the performance of these duties, to be regarded as active belligerents. They must, therefore, neither be shot nor captured; on the contrary, everything must be done to assure the performance of their task and to permit their return on its conclusion.

But it is a fundamental condition of this procedure:

1. That the envoy be quite distinguishable as such by means of universally recognized and well-known marks; distinguishable both by sight and by hearing (flags of truce, white flags, or, if need be, white pocket-handkerchiefs) and signals (horns or bugles).
2. That the envoy behave peaceably, and
3. That he does not abuse his position in order to commit any unlawful act.

Of course any contravention of the last two conditions puts an end to his inviolability; it may justify his immediate capture, and, in extreme cases (espionage, hatching of plots), his condemnation by military law. Should the envoy abuse his mission for purposes of observation, whereby the army he is visiting is imperiled, then also he may be detained, but not longer than is necessary. In all cases of this kind it is recommended that prompt and detailed information be furnished to the head of the other army.

It is the right of every army:

1. To accept or to refuse such envoys. An envoy who is not received must immediately rejoin his own army; he must not, of course, be shot at on his way.
2. To declare that it will not during a fixed period entertain any envoys. Should any appear in spite of this declaration; they cannot claim to be inviolable.
3. To determine in what forms and under what precautions envoys shall be received. The envoys have to submit to any commands even though entailing personal inconvenience such as blindfolding or going out of their way on coming or returning, and such like.

The observance of certain forms in the reception of envoys is of the greatest importance, as a parley may serve as a cloak for obtaining information or for the temporary interruption of hostilities and the like. Such a danger is particularly likely to occur if the combatants have been facing one another, as in the case of a war of positions, for a long time without any particular result. These

The Etiquette of Flags of Truce.

forms are also important because their non-observance, as experience shows, gives rise to recrimi-
nation and charges of violation of the usages of
war. The following may, therefore, be put forward
as the chief rules for the behavior of an envoy and
as the forms to be observed in his reception.

The Envoy.

1. The envoy (who is usually selected as being a
   man skilled in languages and the rules, and is
   mounted on horseback) makes for the enemy's
   outpost or their nearest detachment, furnished
   with the necessary authorization, in the company of a trumpeter and a flag-bearer on
   horseback. If the distance between the two
   outposts of the respective lines is very small,
   then the envoy may go on foot in the company
   of a bugler or a drummer.

His
approach.

2. When he is near enough to the enemy's outposts or their lines to be seen and heard, he
   has the trumpet or bugle blown and the white
   flag unfurled by the bearer. The bearer will
   seek to attract the attention of the enemy's
   outposts or detachments whom he has
   approached, by waving the flag to and fro.

   From this moment the envoy and his company are inviolable, in virtue of a general
   usage of war. The appearance of a flag of
   truce in the middle of a fight, however, binds
   no one to cease fire. Only the envoy and his
   companions are not to be shot at.

3. The envoy now advances with his escort at a slow walk to the nearest posted officer. He must obey the challenge of the enemy's outposts and patrol.

The challenge— "Wer da?"

4. Since it is not befitting to receive an envoy at just that place which he prefers, he has to be ready to be referred to a particular place of admission. He must keep close to the way prescribed for him. It is advisable for the enemy whenever this is possible to give the envoy an escort on the way.

His reception.

5. On arriving at the place indicated, the envoy dismounts along with his attendants; leaves them at a moderate distance behind him, and proceeds on foot to the officer on duty, or highest in command, at that place, in order to make his wishes known.

He dismounts.

6. Intercourse with the enemy's officer must be courteously conducted. The envoy has always to bear in mind the discharge of his mission, to study the greatest circumspection in his conversations, neither to attempt to sound the enemy or to allow himself to be sounded. . . . The best thing is to refuse to enter into any conversation on military matters beforehand.

Let his Yea be Yea, and his Nay, Nay.

7. For less important affairs the officer at the place of admission will possess the necessary instructions, in order either to discharge them himself, or to promise their discharge in a fixed period. But in most cases the decision of

The duty of his Interlocutor.

a superior will have to be taken; in this case the envoy has to wait until the latter arrives.

8. If the envoy has a commission to deal personally with the Commander-in-Chief or a high officer, or if the officer on duty at the place of admission considers it desirable for any reason to send the envoy back, then, if it be necessary, the eyes of the envoy may be blindfolded; to take away his weapons is hardly necessary. If the officer at the place of admission is in any doubt what attitude to adopt towards the requests of the envoy, he will for the time being detain him at his post, and send an intimation to his immediate superior in case the affair appears to him of particular importance, and at the same time to the particular officer to whom the envoy is or should be sent.

The impatient Envoy.

9. If an envoy will not wait, he may be permitted, according to circumstances, to return to his own army if the observation made by him or any communications received can no longer do any harm.

From the foregoing it follows that intercourse with the envoys of an enemy presupposes detailed instructions and a certain intelligence on the part of the officers and men if it is to proceed peaceably. But before all things it must be made clear to the men that the intentional wounding or killing of an envoy is a serious violation of international law, and that even an unfortunate accident which leads to such a violation may have the most disagreeable consequences.

A despatch of Bismarck's of January 9th, 1871, demonstrates by express mention of their names, that twenty-one German envoys were shot by French soldiers while engaged on their mission. Ignorance and defective teaching of the troops may have been the principal reason for this none too excusable behavior. In many cases transgressions on the part of the rawer elements of the army may have occurred, as has been many times offered as an excuse in higher quarters. Nevertheless, this state of affairs makes clear the necessity of detailed instruction and a sharp supervision of the troops by the officers.

The French again.

CHAPTER V

SCOUTS AND SPIES

The Scout. SCOUTING resolves itself into a question of getting possession of important information about the position, strength, plans, etc., of the enemy, and thereby promoting the success of one's own side. The existence of scouting has been closely bound up with warfare from the earliest times; it is to be regarded as an indispensable means of warfare and consequently is undoubtedly permissible. If the scouting takes place publicly by recognizable combatants then it is a perfectly regular form of activity, against which the enemy can only use the regular means of defense, that is to say, killing in battle, and capture. If the scouting takes the form of secret or surreptitious methods, then it is espionage, and is liable to particularly severe and ruthless measures by way of precaution and exemplary punishment—usually death by shooting or hanging. This severe punishment is not inflicted on account of dishonorable disposition on the part of the spy—there need exist nothing of the kind, and the motive for the espionage may arise from the highest patriotism and sentiment of military duty quite as often as from avarice and dishonorable

The Spy and his short shrift.

54

cupidity[1]—but principally on account of the particular danger which lies in such secret methods. It is
as it were a question of self-defense.

Having regard to this severe punishment introduced by the usages of war, it is necessary to
define the conception of espionage and of spies as
precisely as possible.

A spy was defined by the German army staff in
1870 as one "who seeks to discover by clandestine
methods, in order to favor the enemy, the position
of troops, camps, etc.; on the other hand enemies
who are soldiers are only to be regarded as spies if
they have violated the rules of military usages, by
denial or concealment of their military character."

What is a Spy?

The Brussels Declaration of 1874 defines the
conception as follows: "By a spy is to be understood he who clandestinely or by illicit pretenses
enters or attempts to enter into places in the possession of the enemy with the intention of obtaining information to be brought to the knowledge of
the other side." The Hague Conference puts it in
the same way.

The emphasis in both declarations is to be laid
on the idea of "secrecy" or "deception." If regular
combatants make enquiries in this fashion, for

Of the essentials of Espionage.

---

[1] To judge espionage with discrimination according to motives does not
seem to be feasible in war. "Whether it be a patriot who devotes himself, or a
wretch who sells himself, the danger they run at the hands of the enemy will
be the same. One will respect the first and despise the second, but one will
shoot both."—*Quelle* I, 126. This principle is very ancient. As early as 1780 a
North-American court-martial condemned Major André, an Englishman, to
death by hanging, and in vain did the English Generals intercede for him, in
vain did he plead himself, that he be shot as a soldier.

example in disguise, then they also come under the category of spies, and can lawfully be treated as such. Whether the espionage was successful or not makes no difference. The motive which has prompted the spy to accept his commission, whether noble or ignoble, is, as we have already said, indifferent; likewise, whether he has acted on his own impulse or under a commission from his own State or army. The military jurisdiction in this matter cuts across the territorial principle and that of allegiance, in that it makes no difference whether the spy is the subject of the belligerent country or of another State.

It is desirable that the heavy penalty which the spy incurs should be the subject not of mere suspicion but of actual proof of existence of the offense, by means of a trial, however summary (if the swift course of the war permits), and therefore the death penalty will not be enforced without being preceded by a judgment.

Accessories are Principals.

Participation in espionage, favoring it, harboring a spy, are equally punishable with espionage itself.

CHAPTER VI

DESERTERS AND RENEGADES

THE difference between these two is this—the first class are untrue to the colors, their intention being to withdraw altogether from the conflict, to leave the seat of war, and, it may be, to escape into a country outside it; but the second class go over to the enemy in order to fight in his ranks against their former comrades. According to the general usages of war, deserters and renegades, if they are caught, are to be subjected to martial law and may be punished with death.

The Deserter is faithless and the Renegade false.

Although some exponents of the laws of war claim that deserters and renegades should be handed back to one's opponent, and on the other hand exactly the opposite is insisted on by others, namely, the obligation to accept them—all we can say is that a soldier cannot admit any such obligation.

Deserters and renegades weaken the power of the enemy, and therefore to hand them over is not in the interest of the opposite party, and as for the right to accept them or reject them, that is a matter for one's own decision.

But both may be useful.

CHAPTER VII

CIVILIANS IN THE TRAIN OF AN ARMY

"Followers." IN the train of an army it is usual to find, temporarily or permanently, a mass of civilians who are indispensable to the satisfaction of the wants of officers and soldiers or to the connection of the army with the native population. To this category belong all kinds of contractors, carriers of charitable gifts, artists, and the like, and, above all, newspaper correspondents whether native or foreign. If they fall into the hands of the enemy, they have the right, should their detention appear desirable, to be treated as prisoners of war, assuming that they are in possession of an adequate authorization.

For all these individuals, therefore, the possession of a pass issued by the military authorities concerned, in accordance with the forms required by international intercourse, is an indispensable necessity, in order that in the case of a brush with the enemy, or of their being taken captive they may be recognized as occupying a passive position and may not be treated as spies.[1]

---

[1] The want of an adequate authorization led in 1874 to the shooting of the Prussian newspaper correspondent Captain Schmidt by the Carlists, which raised a great outcry. Schmidt was armed with a revolver, with maps of the seat of war, and also with plans and sketches of the Carlists' positions, as against which he had only an ordinary German passport as a Prussian Captain

In the grant of these authorizations the utmost circumspection should be shown by the military authorities; this privilege should only be extended to those whose position, character, and intentions are fully known, or for whom trustworthy persons will act as sureties.

This circumspection must be observed most scrupulously in the case of newspaper correspondents whether native or foreign. Since the component parts of a modern army are drawn from all grades of the population, the intervention of the Press for the purpose of intellectual intercourse between the army and the population at home can no longer be dispensed with. The army also derives great advantages from this intellectual intercourse; it has had to thank the stimulus of the Press in recent campaigns for an unbroken chain of benefits, quite apart from the fact that news of the war in the newspapers is a necessity for every soldier. The importance of this intervention, and on the other hand the dangers and disadvantages which may arise from its misuse, make it obviously necessary that the military authorities should control the whole of the Press when in the field. In what follows we shall briefly indicate the chief rules which are customary, in the modern usages of war, as regards giving permission to newspaper correspondents.

The War Correspondent: his importance. His presence is desirable.

---

and was seized within the Carlists' outpost, and since he could not defend himself, verbally, on account of his ignorance of the Spanish language, he was convicted as a spy by court-martial and shot.

The ideal
War Corre-
spondent.

The first thing necessary in a war correspondent is a sense of honor; in other words, he must
be trustworthy. Only a man who is known to be
absolutely trustworthy, or who can produce a most
precise official certificate or references from unim-
peachable persons, can be granted permission to
attach himself to headquarters.

An honorable correspondent will be anxious to
adhere closely to the duties he owes to his paper
on the one hand, and the demands of the army
whose hospitality he enjoys on the other. To do
both is not always easy, and in many cases tact and
refinement on the part of the correspondent can
alone indicate the right course; a censorship is
proved by experience to be of little use; the certifi-
cates and recommendations required must therefore be explicit as to the possession of these
qualities by the applicant; and according as he possesses them or not his personal position at headquarters and the degree of support extended to
him in the discharge of his duties will be decided.

It is therefore undoubtedly in the interest of the
army as of the Press, that the latter shall only
despatch such representatives as really are equal
to the high demands which the profession of correspondent requires.

The
Etiquette of
the War
Correspon-
dent.

The correspondent admitted on the strength of
satisfactory pledges has therefore to promise on his
word of honor to abide by the following obligations:

1. To spread no news as to the disposition, numbers, or movements of troops, and, moreover, the intentions and plans of the staff, unless he has permission to publish them. (This concerns principally correspondents of foreign newspapers since one's own newspapers are already subject to a prohibition of this kind by the Imperial Press Law of April 7th, 1874.)

2. To report himself on arrival at the headquarters of a division immediately to the commanding officer, and to ask his permission to stay, and to remove himself immediately and without making difficulties if the o.c. deems his presence inexpedient on military grounds.

3. To carry with him always, and to produce on demand, his authorization (certificate, armlet, photograph) and his pass for horses, transport, and servants.

4. To take care that his correspondence and articles are submitted at headquarters.

5. To carry out all instructions of the officers at headquarters who supervise the press.

Contraventions of the orders from headquarters, discretions, and tactlessness, are punished in less serious cases with a caution, in grave cases by expulsion; where the behavior of the correspondent or his correspondence has not amounted to a military offense, and is therefore not punishable by martial law.

A journalist who has been expelled not only loses his privileges but also his passive character; and if he disregards his exclusion he will be held responsible.

Foreign journalists are subject to the same obligations; they must expressly recognize their authority and in case of punishment cannot claim any personal immunity.[2]

Journalists who accompany the army without the permission of the staff, and whose reports therefore cannot be subject to military control, are to be proceeded against with inexorable severity. They are to be expelled ruthlessly as dangerous, since they only get in the way of the troops and devour their subsistence, and may under the mask of friendship do harm to the army.

---

[2] In the Egyptian Campaign in 1882 the English War Office published the following regulations for newspaper correspondents. [The translator does not think it necessary to reproduce these.]

CHAPTER VIII

THE EXTERNAL MARK OF INVIOLABILITY

THOSE persons and objects who in war are to be treated as inviolable must be recognizable by some external mark. Such is the so-called Geneva Cross (a red cross on a white ground) introduced by international agreement.[1]

How to tell a Non-combatant.

Attention is to be attracted in the case of persons by armlets, in the case of buildings by flags, in the case of wagons and other objects by a corresponding paint mark.

If the mark is to receive adequate respect it is essential:

1. That it should be clearly visible and recognizable.
2. That it should only be worn by such persons or attached to such objects as can lawfully claim it.

As to 1. Banners and flags must be sufficiently large to be both distinguishable and recognizable

---

[1] In Turkey, in place of the Red Cross a red half-moon was introduced, and was correspondingly respected by the Russians in the campaign of 1877. Japan, on the contrary, has waived its original objection to the cross.

at a far distance; they are to be so attached that they will not be masked by any national flag that may be near them, otherwise unintentional violations will be unavoidable.

As to 2. Abuse will result in the protective mark being no longer respected, and a further result would be to render illusory, and to endanger, the whole of the Geneva Convention. Measures must therefore be taken to prevent such abuses and to require every member of the army to draw attention to any one who wears these marks without being entitled to do so.[2]

Regulations of international law to prevent and punish misuse of the Red Cross do not exist.[3]

---

[2] That in the war of 1870 the Red Cross was frequently abused on the French side is well known, and has been the subject of documentary proof. The escape of Bourbaki from Metz, under cover of the misuse of the Geneva Convention, proves that even in the highest circles people were not clear as to the binding obligation of International Regulations, and disregarded them in the most frivolous manner.

[3] [But the English legislature has, by the Geneva Convention Act, 1911 (1 and 2 Geo. V, c. 20) made it a statutory offense, punishable on summary conviction by a fine not exceeding £10, to use the heraldic emblem of the Red Cross or the words "Red Cross" for any purpose whatsoever, if the person so using it has not the authority of the Army Council for doing so.—J. H. M.]

CHAPTER IX

WAR TREATIES

In the following pages we have only to do with war treaties in the narrower sense, that is such as are concluded during the war itself and have as their object either the regulation of certain relations during the period of the war, or only an isolated and temporary measure. It is a principle of all such treaties that: *Etiam Zosti fides servanda*. Every agreement is to be strictly observed by both sides in the spirit and in the letter. Should this rule not be observed by one side then the other has the right to regard the treaty as denounced.

That Faith must be kept even with an Enemy.

How a treaty is to be concluded depends on the discretion of those who conclude it. Drafts or models of treaties do not exist.

A.—*Treaties of Exchange*

These have for their object the mutual discharge or exchange of prisoners of war. Whether the opponent will agree to an offer of this kind or not, depends entirely upon himself.

Exchange of Prisoners.

The usual stipulation is: An equal number on both sides. That is only another way of saying that a surplus of prisoners on the one side need not be handed over.

The restitution of a greater number of common soldiers against officers can be stipulated; in that case, the relative value of different grades must be precisely fixed in the treaty.

B.—*Treaties of Capitulation*

Capitulations—they cannot be too meticulous.

The object of these is the surrender of fortresses or strong places as also of troops in the open field. Here again there can be no talk of a generally accepted model. The usages of war have, however, displayed some rules for capitulations, the observance of which is to be recommended:

1. Before any capitulation is concluded, the authority of the Commander who concludes it should be formally and unequivocally authenticated. How necessary a precaution of this kind is, is shown by the capitulations of Rapp at Danzig, and of Gouvion St. Cyr at Dresden, in 1813, which were actually annulled by the refusal of the General Staff of the Allies to ratify them. At the trial of Bazaine the indictment by General Rivière denied the title of the Marshal to conclude a capitulation.

2. If one of the parties to the treaty makes it a condition that the confirmation of the monarch, or the Commander-in-Chief, or even the national assembly is to be obtained, then this circumstance must be made quite clear. Also care is to be taken that in the event of

ratification being refused every advantage that might arise from an ambiguous proceeding on the part of one opponent, be made impossible.

3. The chief effect of a capitulation is to prevent that portion of the enemy's force which capitulates from taking any part in the conflict during the rest of the war, or it may be for a fixed period. The fate of the capitulating troops or of the surrendered fortress differs in different cases.[1] In the Treaty of Capitulation every condition agreed upon both as to time and manner must be expressed in precise and unequivocable words. Conditions which violate the military honor of those capitulated are not permissible according to modern views. Also, if the capitulation is an unconditional one or, to use the old formula, is "at discretion," the victor does not thereby, according to the modern laws of war, acquire a right of life and death over the persons capitulating.

---

[1] How different the conditions of capitulation may be the following examples will show:

Sedan: (1) The French army surrender as prisoners of war. (2) In consideration of the brave defense all Generals, Officers, and Officials occupying the rank of Officers, will receive their freedom so soon as they give their word of honor in writing not to take up arms again until the end of the war, and not to behave in a manner prejudicial to the interests of Germany. The officers and officials who accept these conditions are to keep their arms and their own personal effects. (3) All arms and all war material consisting of flags, eagles, cannons, munitions, etc., are to be surrendered and to be handed over by a French military commission to German commissioners. (4) The fortress of Sedan is to be immediately placed at the disposition (of the Germans) exactly as it stands. (5) The officers who have refused the obligation not to take up arms again, as well as the troops, shall be disarmed and organized according to their regiments or corps to go over in military fashion. The medical staff are without exception to remain behind to look after the wounded. *continued on page 68*

4. Obligations which are contrary to the laws of nations, such as, for example, to fight against one's own Fatherland during the continuation of the war, cannot be imposed upon the troops capitulating. Likewise, also, obligations such as are forbidden them by their own civil or military laws or terms of service, cannot be imposed.

5. Since capitulations are treaties of war they cannot contain, for those contracting them, either rights or duties which extend beyond the period of the war, nor can they include dispositions as to matters of constitutional law such as, for example, a cession of territory.

6. A violation of any of the obligations of the treaty of capitulation justifies an opponent in immediately renewing hostilities without further ceremony.

Of the White Flag.

The external indication of a desire to capitulate is the raising of a white flag. There exists no obligation to cease firing immediately on the appearance of this sign (or to cease hostilities). The

Metz: The capitulation of Metz allowed the disarmed soldiers to keep their knapsacks, effects, and camp equipment, and allowed the officers who preferred to go into captivity, rather than give their word of honor, to take with them their swords, or sabers, and their personal property.

Belfort: The garrison were to receive all the honors of war, to keep their arms, their transport, and their war material. Only the fortress material was to be surrendered.

Bitsch (concluded after the settlement of peace): (1) The garrison retires with all the honors of war, army, banners, artillery, and field pieces. (2) As to siege material and munitions of war a double inventory is to be prepared. (3) In the same way an inventory is to be taken of administrative material. (4) The material referred to in Articles 2 and 3 is to be handed over to the Commandant of the German forces. (5) The archives of the fortress, with the exception of the Commandant's own register, are left behind. (6) The customs officers

attainment of a particular important, possibly decisive, point, the utilization of a favorable moment,
the suspicion of an illicit purpose in raising the
white flag, the saving of time, and the like, may
induce the commanding officer to disregard the
sign until these reasons have disappeared.

If, however, no such considerations exist, then
humanity imposes an immediate cessation of hostilities.

C.—*Safe-conducts*

The object of these is to secure persons or
things from hostile treatment. The usages of war in
this matter furnish the following rules:

Of Safe-conducts.

1. Letters of safe-conduct, for persons, can only
   be given to such persons as are certain to
   behave peaceably and not to misuse them for
   hostile purposes; letters of safe-conduct for
   things are only to be granted under a guaran-
   tee of their not being employed for warlike
   purposes.
2. The safe-conducts granted to persons are personal to them, *i.e.*, they are not available for

---

are to be disarmed and discharged to their own homes. (7) The canteen-
keepers who wish to depart in the ordinary way receive from the local commandant a pass viséd by the German local authorities. (8) The local Commandant remains after the departure of the troops at the disposal of the German
higher authorities till the final settlement; he binds himself on his word of
honor not to leave the fortress. (9) The troops are transported with their horses and baggage by the railroad. (10) The baggage left behind in Bitsch by the
officers of the 1st and 5th Corps will be sent later to an appointed place in
France, two non-commissioned officers remain to guard it and later to send it
back under their supervision.

Nisch (January 10th, 1878): [The translator has not thought it necessary to
reproduce this.]

others. They do not extend to their companions unless they are expressly mentioned.

An exception is only to be made in the case of diplomatists of neutral States, in whose case their usual entourage is assumed to be included even though the members are not specifically named.

3. The safe-conduct is revocable at any time; it can even be altogether withdrawn or not recognized by another superior, if the military situation has so altered that its use is attended with unfavorable consequences for the party which has granted it.

4. A safe-conduct for things on the other hand is not confined to the person of the bearer. It is obvious that if the person of the bearer appears at all suspicious, the safe-conduct can be withdrawn. This can also happen in the case of an officer who does not belong to the authority which granted it. The officer concerned is in this case fully responsible for his proceedings, and should report accordingly.

D.—*Treaties of Armistice*

Of
Armistices.

By armistice is understood a temporary cessation of hostilities by agreement. It rests upon the voluntary agreement of both parties. The object is either the satisfaction of a temporary need such as carrying away the dead, collecting the wounded, and the like, or the preparation of a surrender or of negotiations for peace.

A general armistice must accordingly be distinguished from a local or particular one. The general armistice extends to the whole seat of war, to the whole army, and to allies; it is therefore a formal cessation of the war. A particular armistice on the contrary relates only to a part of the seat of war, to a single part of the opposing army. Thus the armistice of Poischwitz in the autumn of 1813 was a general armistice; that of January 28th, 1871, between Germany and France, was a particular or local one, since the South-Eastern part of the theater of war was not involved.

The right to conclude an armistice, whether general or particular, belongs only to a person in high command, *i.e.*, the Commander-in-Chief. Time to go and obtain the consent of the ruling powers may be wanting. However, if the object of the armistice is to begin negotiations for peace, it is obvious that this can only be determined by the highest authorities of the State.

If an agreement is concluded, then both sides must observe its provisions strictly in the letter and the spirit. A breach of the obligations entered into on the one side can only lead to the immediate renewal of hostilities on the other side.[2] A notifica-

---

[2] Thus, in August, 1813, the numerous trespasses across the frontier on the part of French detachments and patrols led to the entry of the Silesian army into the neutral territory and therewith to a premature commencement of hostilities. Later inquiries show that these trespasses were committed without the orders of a superior and that, therefore, the French staff cannot be reproached with a breach of the compact; but the behavior of Blucher was justified in the circumstances and in any case was based upon good faith.

tion is in this case only necessary if the circumstances admit of the consequent loss of time. If the breach of the armistice is the fault of individuals, then the party to whom they belong is not immediately responsible and cannot be regarded as having broken faith. If, therefore, the behavior of these individuals is not favored or approved by their superiors, there is no ground for a resumption of hostilities. But the guilty persons ought, in such case, to be punished by the party concerned.

Even though the other party does not approve the behavior of the trespassers but is powerless to prevent such trespasses, then the opponent is justified in regarding the armistice as at an end. In order to prevent unintentional violation both parties should notify the armistice as quickly as possible to all, or at any rate to the divisions concerned. Delay in the announcement of the armistice through negligence or bad faith lies, of course, at the door of him whose duty it was to announce it. A violation due to the bad faith of an individual is to be sternly punished.

No one can be compelled to give credit to a communication from the enemy to the effect that an armistice has been concluded; the teaching of military history is full of warnings against lightly crediting such communications.[3]

---

[3] We have here in mind not exclusively intentionally untrue communications, although these also, especially in the Napoleonic war, very frequently occur; very often the untrue communication is made in good faith.

During the fight which took place at Chaffois on January 29th, 1871, when the village was stormed, the cry of Armistice was raised on the French side.

A fixed form for the conclusion of an armistice is not prescribed. A definite and clear declaration is sufficient. It is usual and is advisable to have treaties of this kind in writing in order to exclude all complication, and, in the case of differences of opinion later on, to have a firm foundation to go upon.

During the armistice nothing must occur which could be construed as a continuation of hostilities, the *status quo* must rather be observed as far as possible, provided that the wording of the treaty does not particularize anything to the contrary. On the other hand the belligerents are permitted to do everything which betters or strengthens their position after the expiry of the armistice and the continuation of hostilities. Thus, for example, troops may unhesitatingly be exercised, fresh ones recruited, arms and munitions manufactured, and food supplies brought up, troops shifted and reenforcements brought on the scene. Whether destroyed or damaged fortifications may also be restored is a question to which different answers are given by influential teachers of the law of nations. It is best settled by express agreement in

---

A French officer of the General Staff communicated to the Commander of the 14th Division by the presentation of a written declaration the news of an armistice concluded at Versailles for the whole of France. The document presented, which was directed by the Commander-in-Chief of the French Army in the East, General Clinchant, to the Commander of the French Division engaged at Chaffois, ran as follows:

"An armistice of twenty-one days has been signed on the 27th. I have this evening received the official news. Cease fire in consequence and inform the enemy, according to the forms followed in war, that the armistice exists and that you are charged to bring it to his knowledge.

(*Signed*) CLINCHANT."
continued on page 74

concrete cases, and so with the revictualing of a
besieged fortress.

As regards its duration, an armistice can be concluded either for a determined or an undetermined
period, and with or without a time for giving notice.
If no fixed period is agreed upon, then hostilities
can be recommenced at any time. This, however, is
to be made known to the enemy punctually, so that
the resumption does not represent a surprise. If a
fixed time is agreed on, then hostilities can be
recommenced the very moment it expires, and
without any previous notification. The commencement of an armistice is, in the absence of an
express agreement fixing another time, to date
from the moment of its conclusion; the armistice
expires at dawn of the day to which it extends.
Thus an armistice made to last until January 1st
comes to an end on the last hour of December 31st,
and a shorter armistice with the conclusion of the

Pontarlier, January, 29th, 1871.

Of the conclusion of this armistice no one on the German side had any
knowledge. None the less hostilities ceased for the time being, pending the decision of the higher authorities. Since on the enemy's side it was asserted that
a portion of the French troops in Chaffois had been made prisoners after the
news of the existence of the armistice was communicated, and the order to
cease fire had been given, some thousand French prisoners were set free again
in recognition of this possibility, and the arms which had been originally kept
back from them were later restored to them again. When the proceedings at
Chaffois were reported, General von Manteuffel decided on the 30th January
as follows:

"The news of an armistice for the Army of the South is false; the operations
are to be continued, and the gentlemen in command are on no other condition
to negotiate with the enemy than that of laying down their arms. All other negotiations are, without any cessation of hostilities, to be referred to the Commander-in-Chief."

number of hours agreed upon thus, for example, an armistice concluded on May 1st at 6 P.M. for 48 hours last until May 3rd at 6 P.M.

PART II

CHAPTER I

RIGHTS AND DUTIES OF THE INHABITANTS

IT has already been shown in the introduction that war concerns not merely the active elements, but that also the passive elements are involved in the common suffering, *i.e.*, the inhabitants of the occupied territory who do not belong to the army. Opinions as to the relations between these peaceable inhabitants of the occupied territory and the army in hostile possession have fundamentally altered in the course of the last century. Whereas in earlier times the devastation of the enemy's territory, the destruction of property, and, in some cases indeed, the carrying away of the inhabitants into bondage or captivity, were regarded as a quite natural consequence of the state of war, and whereas in later times milder treatment of the inhabitants took place although destruction and annihilation as a military resource still continued to be entertained, and the right of plundering the

The Civil Population is not to be regarded as an enemy.

77

private property of the inhabitants remained completely unlimited—to-day, the universally prevalent idea is that the inhabitants of the enemy's territory are no longer to be regarded, generally speaking, as enemies. It will be admitted, as a matter of law, that the population is, in the exceptional circumstances of war, subjected to the limitations, burdens, and measures of compulsion conditioned by it, and owes obedience for the time being to the power *de facto*, but may continue to exist otherwise undisturbed and protected as in time of peace by the course of law.

They must not be molested.

It follows from all this, as a matter of right, that, as regards the personal position of the inhabitants of the occupied territory, neither in life or in limb, in honor or in freedom, are they to be injured, and that every unlawful killing; every bodily injury, due to fraud or negligence; every insult; every disturbance of domestic peace; every attack on family, honor, and morality and, generally, every unlawful and outrageous attack or act of violence, are just as strictly punishable as though they had been committed against the inhabitants of one's own land. There follows, also, as a right of the inhabitants of the enemy territory, that the invading army can only limit their personal independence in so far as the necessity of war unconditionally demands it, and that any infliction that needlessly goes beyond this is to be avoided.

As against this right, there is naturally a corre- Their duty.
sponding duty on the part of the inhabitants to
conduct themselves in a really peaceable manner,
in no wise to participate in the conflict, to abstain
from every injury to the troops of the power in
occupation, and not to refuse obedience to the
enemy's government. If this presumption is not ful-
filled, then there can no longer be any talk of violations of the immunities of the inhabitants, rather
they are treated and punished strictly according to
martial law.

The conception here put forward as to the rela- Of the
humanity
of the
Germans
and the
barbarity
of the
French.
tion between the army and the inhabitants of an
enemy's territory, corresponds to that of the German Staff in the years 1870–71. It was given
expression in numerous proclamations, and in still
more numerous orders of the day, of the German
Generals. In contrast to this the behavior of the
French authorities more than once betrays a complete ignorance of the elementary rules of the law
of nations, alike in their diplomatic accusations
against the Germans and in the words used
towards their own subjects. Thus, on the outbreak
of the war, a threat was addressed to the Grand
Duchy of Baden, not only by the French Press but
also officially (*von amtlicher Stelle*),[1] "that even
its women would not be protected." So also horses

---

[1] [It will be observed that no authority is given for this statement.—J. H. M.]

of Prussian officers, who had been shot by the
peasants, were publicly put up to auction by the
murderers. So also the Franctireurs threatened the
inhabitants of villages occupied by the Germans
that they would be shot and their houses burnt
down if they received the enemy in their houses or
"were to enter into intercourse with them." So also
the prefect of the Cote d'Or, in an official circular
of November 21st, urges the sub-prefects and may-
ors of his Department to a systematic pursuit of
assassination, when he says: "The Fatherland does
not demand of you that you should assemble *en
masse* and openly oppose the enemy, it only
expects that three or four determined men should
leave the village every morning and conceal themselves in a place indicated by nature, from which,
without danger, they can shoot the Prussians;
above all, they are to shoot at the enemy's mounted
men whose horses they are to deliver up at the
principal place of the Arrondissement. I will award
a bonus to them (for the delivery of such horses),
and will publish their heroic deed in all the newspapers of Department, as well as in the *Moniteur.*"
But this conception of the relation between the
inhabitants and the hostile army not only pos-
sessed the minds of the provincial authorities but
also the central government at Tours itself, as is
clear from the fact that it held it necessary to stig-
matize publicly the members of the municipal com-

mission at Soissons who, after an attempt on the life of a Prussian sentry by an unknown hand, prudently warned their members against a repetition of such outrages, when it [the central government] ordered "that the names of the men who had lent themselves to the assistance and interpretation of the enemy's police be immediately forthcoming."[2] And if, on the French side, the proclamation of General von Falckenstein is cited as a proof of similar views on the German side—the proclamation wherein the dwellers on the coast of the North Sea and the Baltic are urged to participate in the defense of the coast, and are told: "Let every Frenchman who sets foot on your coast be forfeit"—as against this all that need be said is that this incitement, as is well known, had no effect in Germany and excited the greatest surprise and was properly condemned.

Having thus developed the principles governing the relation between the hostile army and the inhabitants, we will now consider somewhat more closely the duties of the latter and the burdens which, in a given case, it is allowable to impose upon it. Obviously a precise enumeration of every kind of service which may be demanded from them is impossible, but the following of the most frequent occurrence are:

What the Invader may do.

---

[2] See as to this: *Rolin-Jacquemyns*, II, 34; and Dahn, *Der Deutsch-Französische Krieg und das Völkerrecht.*

1. Restriction of post, railway and letter communication, supervision, or, indeed, total prohibition of the same.
2. Limitation of freedom of movement within the
   country, prohibition to frequent certain parts
   of the seat of war, or specified places.
3. Surrender of arms.
4. Obligation to billet the enemy's soldiers; prohibition of illumination of windows at night
   and the like.
5. Production of conveyances.
6. Performance of work on streets, bridges,
   trenches (*Gräben*), railways, buildings, etc.
7. Production of hostages.

As to 1, the necessity of interrupting, in many
cases, railway, postal, and telegraph communication, of stopping them or, at the least, stringently
supervising them, hardly calls for further proof.
Human feeling on the part of the commanding officer will know what limits to fix, where the needs
of the war and the necessities of the population
permit of mutual accommodation.

As to 2, if according to modern views no inhabitant of occupied territory can be compelled to participate directly in the fight against his own
Fatherland, so, conversely, he can be prevented
from reenforcing his own army. Thus the German
staff in 1870, where it had acquired authority, in

particular in Alsace-Lorraine, sought to prevent the entrance of the inhabitants into the French army, even as in the Napoleonic wars the French authorities sought to prevent the adherence of the States of the Rhine Confederation to the army of the Allies.

The view that no inhabitant of occupied territory can be compelled to participate directly in the struggle against his own country is subject to an exception by the general usages of war which must be recorded here: the calling up and employment of the inhabitants as guides on unfamiliar ground. However much it may ruffle human feeling, to compel a man to do harm to his own Fatherland, and indirectly to fight his own troops, none the less no army operating in an enemy's country will altogether renounce this expedient.[3]

A man may be compelled to betray his Country.

But a still more severe measure is the compulsion of the inhabitants to furnish information about their own army, its strategy, its resources, and its military secrets. The majority of writers of all nations are unanimous in their condemnation of this measure. Nevertheless it cannot be entirely dispensed with; doubtless it will be applied with regret, but the argument of war will frequently make it necessary.[4]

And Worse.

As to 5 and 6, the summoning of the inhabitants to supply vehicles and perform works has also

Of forced labor.

---

[3] [See Editor's Introduction for criticism of this brutality.—J. H. M.]

[4] [*Ibid.*]

been stigmatized as an unjustifiable compulsion upon the inhabitants to participate in "Military operations." But it is clear that an officer can never allow such far-reaching extension of this conception, since otherwise every possibility of compelling work would disappear, while every kind of work to be performed in war, every vehicle to be furnished in any connection with the conduct of war, is or may be bound up with it. Thus the argument of war must decide. The German Staff, in the War of 1870, moreover, rarely made use of compulsion in order to obtain civilian workers for the performance of necessary works. It paid high wages and, therefore, almost always had at its disposal sufficient offers. This procedure should, therefore, be maintained in future cases. The provision of a supply of labor is best arranged through the medium of the local authorities. In case of refusal of workers punishment can, of course, be inflicted.

Of a certain harsh measure and its justification.

Therefore the conduct of the German civil commissioner, Count Renard—so strongly condemned by French jurists and jurists with French sympathies—who, in order to compel labor for the necessary repair of a bridge, threatened, in case of further refusal, after stringent threats of punishment had not succeeded in getting the work done, to punish the workers by shooting some of them, was in accordance with the actual laws of war; *the main thing was that it attained its object*, without its being necessary to practise it. The accusation made by the French that, on the German side, Frenchmen were compelled to labor at the siege works before Strassburg, has been proved to be incorrect.

7. By hostages are understood those persons who, as security or bail for the fulfilment of treaties, promises or other claims, are taken or detained by the opposing State or its army. Their provision has been less usual in recent wars, as a result of which some Professors of the law of nations have wrongly decided that the taking of hostages has disappeared from the practise of civilized nations. As a matter of fact it was frequently practised in the Napoleonic wars; also in the wars of 1848, 1849, and 1859 by the Austrians in Italy; in 1864 and 1866 by Prussia; in the campaigns of the French in Algiers; of the Russians in the Caucasus; of the English in their Colonial wars, as being the usual thing. The unfavorable criticisms of it by the German Staff in isolated cases is therefore to be referred to different grounds of applied expedients.[5]

Hostages.

A new application of "hostage-right" was practised by the German Staff in the war of 1870, when it compelled leading citizens from French towns

A "harsh and cruel" measure.

---

[5] For example, the carrying off of forty leading citizens from Dijon and neighboring towns as reprisals against the making prisoners of the crew of German merchantmen by the French (undoubtedly contrary to the law of nations), the pretense being that the crews could serve to reenforce the German navy (a pretense strikingly repudiated by Bismarck's Notes of October 4th and November 16th, 1870). Lüder, *Das Landkriegsrecht*, p. 111.

and villages to accompany trains and locomotives in order to protect the railways communications which were threatened by the people. Since the lives of peaceable inhabitants were without any fault on their part thereby exposed to grave danger, every writer outside Germany has stigmatized this measure as contrary to the law of nations and as unjustified towards the inhabitants of the country. As against this unfavorable criticism it must be pointed out that this measure, which was also recognized on the German side as harsh and cruel, was only resorted to after declarations and instructions of the occupying[6] authorities had proved ineffective, and that in the particular circumstance it was the only method which promised to be effective against the doubtless unauthorized, indeed the criminal, behavior of a fanatical population.

But it was "successful."

Herein lies its justification under the laws of war, but still more in the fact that it proved completely successful, and that wherever citizens were thus carried on the trains (whether result was due to the increased watchfulness of the communes or to the immediate influence on the population), the security of traffic was restored.[7]

To protect oneself against attack and injuries from the inhabitants and to employ ruthlessly the

---

[6] Proclamation of the Governor-General of Alsace, and to the same effect the Governor-General of Lorraine of October 18th, 1870.

[7] See Loning, *Die Verwaltung des General-gouvernements en Elsass*, p. 107.

necessary means of defense and intimidation is obviously not only a right but indeed a duty of the staff of the army. The ordinary law will in this matter generally not suffice, it must be supplemented by the law of the enemy's might. Martial law and courts-martial must take the place of the ordinary jurisdiction.[8]

To Martial law are subject in particular:

1. All attacks, violations, homicides, and robberies, by soldiers belonging to the army of occupation.
2. All attacks on the equipment of this army, its supplies, ammunition, and the like.
3. Every destruction of communication, such as bridges, canals, roads, railways and telegraphs.
4. War rebellion and war treason.

Only the fourth point requires explanation.

By war rebellion is to be understood the taking up of arms by the inhabitants against the occupation; by war treason on the other hand the injury or imperiling of the enemy's authority through deceit or through communication of news to one's own army as to the disposition, movement, and

War Rebellion.

---

[8] For a state of war the provisions of the Prussian Law of June 4th, 1861, still hold good to-day. According to this law all the inhabitants of the territory in a state of siege are subject to military courts in regard to certain punishable proceedings.

intention, etc., of the army in occupation, whether the person concerned has come into possession of his information by lawful or unlawful means (*i.e.*, by espionage).

Against both of these only the most ruthless measures are effective. Napoleon wrote to his brother Joseph, when, after the latter ascended the throne of Naples, the inhabitants of lower Italy made various attempts at revolt: "The security of your dominion depends on how you behave in the conquered province. Burn down a dozen places which are not willing to submit themselves. Of course, not until you have first looted them; my soldiers must not be allowed to go away with their hands empty. Have three to six persons hanged in every village which has joined the revolt; pay no respect to the cassock. Simply bear in mind how I dealt with them in Piacenza and Corsica." The Duke of Wellington, in, 1814, threatened the South of France; "he will, if leaders of factions are supported, burn the villages and have their inhabitants hanged." In the year 1815, he issued the following proclamation: "All those who after the entry of the (English) army into France leave their dwellings and all those who are found in the service of the usurper will be regarded as adherents of his and as enemies; their property will be used for the maintenance of the army." "These are the expressions in the one case of one of the great masters of war and of the dominion founded upon war power, and in the other, of a commander-in-chief who elsewhere had carried the protection of private property in hostile lands to the extremest possible limit. Both men as soon as a popular rising takes place resort to terrorism."[9]

A particular kind of war treason, which must be briefly gone into here, inasmuch as the views of the jurists about it differ very strongly from the usages of war, is the case of deception in leading the way, perpetrated in the form of deliberate guiding of the enemy's troops by an inhabitant on a false or disadvantageous road. If he has offered his services, then the fact of his treason is quite clear, but also in case he was forced to act as guide his offense cannot be judged differently, for he owed obedience to the power in occupation, he durst in no case perpetrate an act of open resistance and positive harm but should have, if the worst came to the worst, limited himself to passive disobedience, and he must therefore bear the consequence.[10]

"War Treason" and Unwilling Guides.

However intelligible the inclination to treat and to judge an offense of this kind from a milder standpoint may appear, none the less the leader of the troops thus harmed cannot do otherwise than

Another deplorable necessity.

---

[9] J. von Hartmann, *Kritische Versuche*, II, p. 73.

[10] Lüder, *Das Landkriegsrecht*, p. 103.

punish the offender with death, since only by harsh measures of defense and intimidation can the repetition of such offenses be prevented. In this case a court-martial must precede the infliction of the penalty. The court-martial must however be on its guard against imputing hastily a treasonable intent to the guide. The punishment of misdirection requires in every case proof of evil intention.

Also it is not allowable to diplomatic agents to make communications from the country which they inhabit during the war to any side as to the military situation or proceedings. Persons contravening this universally recognized usage of war may be immediately expelled or in the case of great danger arrested.

CHAPTER II

PRIVATE PROPERTY IN WAR

SINCE, according to the law of nations and the law of war to-day, war makes enemies of States and not of private persons, it follows that every arbitrary devastation of the country and every destruction of private property, generally speaking every unnecessary (*i.e.*, not required by the necessity of war) injury to alien property is contrary to the law of nations. Every inhabitant of the territory occupied is therefore to be protected alike in his person and in his property.

Of Private Property and its immunities.

In this sense spoke King William to the French at the beginning of the Campaign of 1870: "I wage war with the French soldiers and not with the French citizens. The latter will therefore continue to enjoy security for their person and their goods, so long as they do not by hostile undertakings against German troops deprive me of the right to afford them my protection."

The question stands in quite another position if the necessity of war demands the requisition of the stranger's property, whether public or private. In this case of course every sequestration, every temporary or permanent deprivation, every use, every injury and all destruction are permitted.

The following principles therefore result:

1. Prohibited unconditionally are all aimless destructions, devastations, burnings, and ravages of the enemy's country. The soldier who practises such things is punished as an offender according to the appropriate laws.[1]
2. Permissible on the other hand are all destructions and injuries dictated by military considerations; and, indeed,

> (*a*) All demolitions of houses and other buildings, bridges, railways, and telegraphic establishments, due to the necessity of military operations.
>
> (*b*) All injuries which are required through military movements in the country or for earthworks for attack or defense.

Hence the double rule: No harm must be done, not even the very slightest, which is not dictated by military consideration; every kind of harm may be done, even the very utmost, which the conduct of war requires or which comes in the natural course of it.

Whether the natural justification exists or not is a subject for decision in each individual case. The

---

[1] Obviously we are only speaking of a war between civilized people since, in the case of savages and barbarians, humanity is not advanced very far, and one cannot act otherwise toward them than by devastation of their grain fields, driving away their herds, taking of hostages, and the like.

answer to this question lies entirely in the power of the Commanding Officer, from whose conscience our times can expect and demand as far-reaching humanity as the object of war permits.

On similar principles must be answered the question as to the temporary use of property, dispositions as to houses and the like: no inhabitant of the occupied territory is to be disturbed in the use and free disposition of his property, on the other hand the necessity of war justifies the most far-reaching disturbance, restriction, and even imperiling of his property. In consequence there are permitted:

1. Requisitions of houses and their furniture for the purpose of billeting troops.
2. Use of houses and their furniture for the care of the sick and wounded.
3. Use of buildings for observation, shelter, defense, fortification, and the like.

Whether the property owners are subjects of the occupied territory or of a Foreign State is a matter of complete indifference; also the property of the Sovereign and his family is subject to no exception, although to-day it is usually treated with courtesy.

The conception of the inviolability of private property here depicted was shared by the Germans

Of German behavior.

in 1870 and was observed. If on the French side
statements to the contrary are even to-day given
expression, they rest either on untruth or exagger-
ation. It certainly cannot be maintained that no
illegitimate violations of private property by individuals ever occurred. But that kind of thing can
never be entirely avoided even among the most
highly cultivated nations, and the best disciplined
armies. In every case the strictest respect for private property was enjoined[2] upon the soldiers by
the German Military Authorities after crossing the
frontier, and strong measures were taken in order
to make this injunction effective; the property of
the French was indeed, as might be shown in
numerous cases, protected against the population
itself, and was even in several cases saved at the
risk of our own lives.[3]

The gentle Hun and the looking-glass.

In like manner arbitrary destructions and ravages of buildings and the like did not occur on the

---

[2] Army Order of August 8th, 1870, on crossing the frontier: "Soldiers! the pursuit of the enemy who has been thrust back after bloody struggles has already
led a great part of our army across the frontier. Several corps will to-day and
tomorrow set foot upon French soil. I expect that the discipline by which you
have hitherto distinguished yourselves will be particularly observed on the
enemy's territory. We wage no war against the peaceable inhabitants of the
country; it is rather the duty of every honor-loving soldier to protect private
property and not to allow the good name of our army to be soiled by a single
example of bad discipline. I count upon the good spirit which animates the
army, but at the same time also upon the sternness and circumspection of all
leaders.

Headquarters, Homburg, August 8th, 1870.
(*Signed*) WILHELM."

[3] "It is well known that the vineyards in France were guarded and protected
by the German troops, but the same thing happened in regard to the art treasures of Versailles, and the German soldiers protected French property at the
risk of their lives against the incendiary bombs of the Paris Commune."—
Lüder, *Landkriegsrecht*, p. 118.

German side where they were not called forth by
the behavior of the inhabitants themselves. They
scarcely ever occurred except where the inhabitants had foolishly left their dwellings and the soldiers were excited by closed doors and want of
food. "If the soldier finds the doors of his quarters
shut, and the food intentionally concealed or
buried, then necessity impels him to burst open
the doors and to track the stores, and he then, in
righteous anger, destroys a mirror, and with the
broken furniture heats the stove."[4]

If minor injuries explain themselves in this
fashion in the eyes of every reasonable and thinking man, so the result of a fundamental and unprej-
udiced examination has shown that the
destructions and ravages on a greater scale, which
were made a reproach against the German Army,
have in no case overstepped the necessity prescribed by the military situation. Thus the much
talked of and, on the French side, enormously
exaggerated, burning down of twelve houses in
Bazeilles, together with the shooting of an inhabitant, were completely justified and, indeed, in harmony with the laws of war; indeed one may
maintain that the conduct of the inhabitants would
have been called for the complete destruction of
the village and the condemnation of all the adult
inhabitants by martial law.

---

[4] Bluntschli, *Völkerrecht*, sec. 652.

CHAPTER III

BOOTY AND PLUNDERING

Booty. IN section 1, the inhabitant of the enemy's territory was described as a subject of legal rights and duties, who, so far as the nature of war allows, may continue to live protected as in time of peace by the course of law; further, in section 2, property, whether it be public or private, was likewise, so far as war allows it, declared to be inviolable—it therefore follows logically that there can exist no right to the appropriation of the property, *i.e.*, a right to booty or plundering. Opinions as to this have, in the course of the last century, undergone a complete change; the earlier unlimited right of appropriation in war is to-day recognized in regard to public property as existing only in defined circumstances.

In the development of the principles recognized to-day we have to distinguish.

1. State property and unquestionably:
   (*a*) immovable,[1]
   (*b*) movable.[1]

---

[1] [These terms are translated literally. They are roughly equivalent to the English distinction between "real" and "personal" property.—J. H. M.]

2. Private property:
  (*a*) immovable,
  (*b*) movable.

Immovable State property is now no longer for-feited as booty; it may, however, be used if such use is in the interests of military operation, and even destroyed, or temporarily administered. While in the wars of the First French Empire, Napoleon, in numerous cases, even during the war itself, disposed of the public property of the enemy (domains, castles, mines, salt-works) in favor of his Marshals and diplomatists, to-day an appropri-ation of this kind is considered by international opinion to be unjustified and, in order to be valid, requires a formal treaty between the conqueror and the conquered.

The Military Government by the army of occu-pation is only a Usufructuary *pro tempore*. It must, therefore, avoid every purposeless injury, it has no right to sell or dispose of the property. According to this juristic view the military administration of the conqueror disposes of the public revenue and taxes which are raised in the occupied territory, with the understanding, however, that the regular and unavoidable expenses of administration con-tinue to be defrayed. The military authority con-trols the railways and telegraphs of the enemy's State, but here also it possesses only the right of

The State realty may be used but must not be wasted.

use and has to give back the material after the end of the war. In the administration of the State forests, it is not bound to follow the mode of administration of the enemy's Forest authorities, but it must not damage the woods by excessive cutting, still less may it cut them down altogether.

State Personalty is at the mercy of the victor.

Movable State property on the other hand can, according to modern views, be unconditionally appropriated by the conqueror.

This includes public funds,[2] arms, and munition stores, magazines, transport, material supplies useful for the war and the like. Since the possession of things of this kind is of the highest importance for the conduct of the war, the conqueror is justified in destroying and annihilating them if he is not able to keep them.

On the other hand an exception is made as to all objects which serve the purposes of religious worship, education, the sciences and arts, charities and nursing. Protection must therefore be extended to: the property of churches and schools, of libraries and museums, of almshouses and hospitals. The usual practise of the Napoleonic campaigns[3] so ruthlessly resorted to of carrying off art treasures, antiquities, and whole collections, in order to incorporate them in one's own art gal-

---

[2] To be entirely distinguished from municipal funds which are regarded as private property.

[3] How sensitive, indeed, how utterly sentimental, public opinion has become to-day in regard to this question, is shown by the attitude of the French and German Press in regard to some objects of art carried away from China.

leries, is no longer allowed by the law of nations to-day.[4]

Immovable private property may well be the object of military operations and military policy, but cannot be appropriated as booty, nor expended for fiscal or private purposes of acquisition. This also includes, of course, the private property of the ruling family, in so far as it really possesses this character and is not Crown Lands, whose fruits are expended as a kind of Civil List or serve to supplement the same.

Private realty.

Movable private property, finally, which in earlier times was the undeniable booty of the conqueror, is to-day regarded as inviolable. The carrying off of money, watches, rings, trinkets, or other objects of value, is therefore to be regarded as criminal robbery and to be punished accordingly.

Private personalty.

The appropriation of private property is regarded as partially permissible in the case of those objects which the conquered combatant carries on his own person. Still here also, opinions against the practise make it clear that the taking away of objects of value, money, and such-like is not permissible, and only those required for the equipment of troops are declared capable of appropriation.

---

[4] As to booty in the shape of horses, the Prussian instructions say: "Horses taken as booty belong to the State and are therefore to be handed over to the horse depot. For every horse which is still serviceable he who has captured it receives a bonus of 18 dollars out of the exchequer, and for every unserviceable horse half this sum."

The recognition of the inviolability of private property does not of course exclude the sequestration of such objects as can, although they are private property, at the same time be regarded as of use in war. This includes, for example, warehouses of supplies, stores of arms in factories, depots of conveyances or other means of traffic, as bicycles, motor cars, and the like, or other articles likely to be of use with advantage to the army, as telescopes, etc. In order to assure to the possessors compensation from their government, equity enjoins that a receipt be given for the sequestration.

"Choses in action."

Logically related to movable property are the so-called "incorporeal things." When Napoleon, for example, appropriated the debts due to the Elector of Hesse and thus compelled the Elector's debtors to pay their debts to him; when he furthermore in 1807 allowed the debts owed by the inhabitants of the Duchy of Warsaw to Prussian banks and other public institutions, and indeed even to private persons in Prussia, to be assigned by the King of Prussia, and then sold them to the King of Saxony for 200 million francs, this was, according to the modern view, nothing better than robbery.

Plundering is wicked.

Plundering is to be regarded as the worst form of appropriation of a stranger's property. By this is to be understood the robbing of inhabitants by the employment of terror and the abuse of a military superiority. The main point of the offense thus con-

sists in the fact that the perpetrator, finding himself in the presence of the browbeaten owner, who
feels defenseless and can offer no opposition,
appropriates things, such as food and clothing,
which he does not want for his own needs. It is not
plundering but downright burglary if a man pilfers
things out of uninhabited houses or at times when
the owner is absent.

Plundering is by the law of nations to-day to be
regarded as invariably unlawful. If it may be difficult sometimes in the very heat of the fight to
restrain excited troops from trespasses, yet unlawful plundering, extortion, or other violations of
property, must be most sternly punished, it matters
not whether it be done by members of unbroken
divisions of troops or by detached soldiers, so-
called marauders, or by the "hyenas of the battlefield." To permit such transgressions only leads, as
experience shows, to bad discipline and the
demoralization of the Army.[5]

In the Franco-Prussian War, plundering and taking of booty were on the German side sternly forbidden. The Articles of War in question were
repeatedly recalled to every soldier just as in time

---

[5] Napoleon, who actually permitted his soldiers to plunder in numerous
cases and in others, at least, did not do his best to prevent it, spoke of it at St.
Helena: "Policy and morality are in complete agreement in their opposition to
pillage. I have meditated a good deal on this subject; I have often been in a position to gratify my soldiers thereby; I would have done it if I had found it advantageous. But nothing is more calculated to disorganize and completely ruin
an army. From the moment he is allowed to pillage, a soldier's discipline is
gone."

of peace, also numerous orders of the day were issued on the part of the higher authorities. Transgressions were ruthlessly punished, in some cases even after the War.

CHAPTER IV

REQUISITIONS AND WAR LEVIES

By requisitions is to be understood the compulsory appropriation of certain objects necessary for the army which is waging war. What things belong to this category is quite undetermined. They were primarily the means to feed man and beast, next to clothe and equip the members of the army, *i.e.*, to substitute clothing and equipment for that which has worn out or become insufficient in view of the altered circumstances and also to supplement it; furthermore, there will be such objects as serve for the transport of necessaries, and finally all objects may be demanded which serve to supply a temporary necessity, such as material and tools for the building of fortifications, bridges, railways and the like. That requisitions of this kind are unconditionally necessary and indispensable for the existence of the army, no one has yet denied; and whether one bases it legally upon necessity or merely upon the might of the stronger is a matter of indifference as far as the practise is concerned. Requisitions.

The right generally recognized by the law of nations of to-day to requisition is a child of the French Revolution and its wars. It is known that as How the docile German learnt the "better way."

103

late as in the year 1806, Prussian battalions
camped close to big stacks of corn and bivouacked
on potato fields without daring to appease their
hunger with the property of the stranger; the
behavior of the French soon taught them a better
way. Every one knows the ruthless fashion in
which the army of the French Republic and of
Napoleon satisfied their wants, but of late opinion
laying stress upon the protection of private property has asserted itself. Since a prohibition of requisitions would, considering what war is, have no
prospect of acceptance under the law of nations,
the demand has been put forward that the objects
supplied should at least be paid for. This idea has
indeed up till now not become a principle of war,
the right of requisitioning without payment exists
as much as ever and will certainly be claimed in
the future by the armies in the field, and also, considering the size of modern armies, must be
claimed; but it has at least become the custom to
requisition with as much forbearance as possible,
and to furnish a receipt for what is taken, the discharge of which is then determined on the conclusion of peace.

To ex-
haust the
country is
deplorable
but we
mean to
do it.

In order to avoid overdoing it, as may easily
happen in the case of requisitions, it is often
arranged that requisitions may never be demanded
by subordinates but only by the higher officers,
and that the local civil authorities shall be

employed for the purpose. It cannot, however, be denied that this is not always possible in war; that on the contrary the leader of a small detachment and in some circumstances even a man by himself may be under the necessity to requisition what is indispensable to him. Article 40 of the Declaration of Brussels requires that the requisitions (being written out) shall bear a direct relation to the capacity and resources of a country, and, indeed, the justification for this condition would be willingly recognized by every one in theory, but it will scarcely ever be observed in practise. In cases of necessity the needs of the army will alone decide, and a man does well generally to make himself familiar with the reflection that, in the changing and stormy course of a war, observance of the orderly conduct of peaceful times is, with the best will, impossible.

In the Franco-Prussian War of 1870 much was requisitioned on the German side. According to the opinion of all impartial writers it was done with moderation and the utmost tenderness for the inhabitants, even if in isolated cases excesses occurred. Receipts were always furnished. Later, in the case of the army on the Meuse, as early as the middle of October requisitions were, wherever it was possible entirely left out of account and everything was paid for in cash. Later proceedings were frequently and indeed studiously conducted with a precise estimate of the value in thalers or francs.[1] "Moreover, military history knows of no campaign in which the victualing of an army at such a distance from home was so largely conducted with its own stores."[2]

"Buccaneering Levies."

By war levies or contributions is to be understood the raising of larger or smaller sums of money from the parishes of the occupied territory. They are thus to be distinguished from requisitions since they do not serve for the satisfaction of a momentary want of the army and consequently can only in the rarest cases be based upon the necessity of war. These levies originated as so-called "*Brandschatzungen,*" *i.e.,* as a ransom from plundering and devastation, and thus constituted, compared with the earlier looting system, a step in the humanizing of war. Since the law of nations to-day no longer recognizes any right to plundering and devastation, and inasmuch as the principle that war is conducted only against States, and not against private persons, is uncontested, it follows logically that levies which can be characterized as simply booty-making or plundering, that is to say, as arbitrary enrichment of the conquerors, are not permitted by modern opinion. The conqueror is, in particular, not justified in recouping himself for the cost of the war by inroads upon the property of

[1] Dahn; *Jahrbuch f. A.u.M.*, III, 1876. Jacquemyns Revue.

[2] Dahn, *ibid.*, III, 1871.

private persons, even though the war was forced upon him.

War levies are therefore only allowed:

1. As a substitute for taxes.
2. As a substitute for the supplies to be furnished as requisitions by the population.
3. As punishments.

As to 1: This rests upon the right of the power in occupation to raise and utilize taxes.

As to 2: In cases where the provision of prescribed objects in a particular district is impossible, and in consequence the deficiency has to be met by purchase in a neighboring district.

As to 3: War levies as a means of punishing individuals or whole parishes were very frequently employed in the Franco-Prussian War. If French writers accuse the German staff of excessive severity in this respect, on the other hand it is to be remarked that the embittered character which the war took on in its latest stage, and the lively participation of the population therein, necessitated the sternest measures. But a money tax, judging by experience, operates, in most cases, on the civil population. The total sum of all the money contributions raised in the War of 1870 may be called a minimum compared with the sums which Napoleon was accustomed to draw from the terri-

tories occupied by him. According to official esti-
mates, havoc amounting to about six milliards of
francs was visited upon the four million inhabitants of Prussia in the years 1807–13.

In regard to the raising of war levies it should
be noted that they should only be decreed by superior officers and only raised with the cooperation
of the local authorities. Obviously an acknowledg-
ment of every sum raised is to be furnished.

1. In the military laws of different countries the
   right of levying contributions is exclusively
   reserved to the Commander-in-Chief.
2. The usual method of raising taxes would, in
   consequence of their slowness, not be in harmony with the demands of the War; usually,
   therefore, the Civil Authorities provide themselves with the necessary money by a loan, the
   repayment of which is provided for later by
   law.

CHAPTER V

ADMINISTRATION OF OCCUPIED TERRITORY

ACCORDING to earlier views right up to the last century, a Government whose army had victoriously
forced itself into the territory of a foreign State
could do exactly as it pleased in the part occupied.
No regard was to be paid to the constitution, laws,
and rights of the inhabitants. Modern times have
now introduced, in this respect, a change in the
dominant conceptions, and have established a certain legal relationship between the inhabitants and
the army of occupation. If, in the following pages,
we develop briefly the principles which are applied
to the government of territory in occupation, it
must none the less be clearly emphasized that the
necessities of war not only allow a deviation from
these principles in many cases but in some circumstances make it a positive duty of the Commander.

How to administer an Invaded Country.

The occupation of a portion of the enemy's territory does not amount to an annexation of it. The
right of the original State authority consequently
remains in existence; it is only suspended when it
comes into collision with the stronger power of
the conqueror during the term of the occupation,
i.e., only for the time being.

But the administration of a country itself cannot be interrupted by war;[1] it is therefore in the interest of the country and its inhabitants themselves, if the conqueror takes it in hand, to let it be carried on either with the help of the old, or, if this is not feasible, through the substitution of the new, authorities.

From this fundamental conception now arises a series of rights and duties of the conqueror on the one side and of the inhabitants on the other.

The Laws remain— with qualification.

Since the conqueror is only the substitute for the real Government, he will have to establish the continuation of the administration of the country with the help of the existing laws and regulations. The issue of new laws, the abolition or alteration of old ones, and the like, are to be avoided if they are not excused by imperative requirements of war; only the latter permit legislation which exceeds the need of a provisional administration. The French Republic, at the end of the eighteenth century, frequently abolished the preexisting constitution in the States conquered by it, and substituted a Republican one, but this is none the less contrary to the law of nations to-day. On the other hand, a restriction of the freedom of the Press, of the right of association, and of public meeting, the

---

[1] The King of Denmark in 1715, whilst Charles XII, after the Battle of Pultawa, stayed for years in Bender, sold the conquered principalities of Bremen and Verden to the King of England, Elector of Hanover, before England had yet declared war on Sweden. This undoubtedly unlawful act of England first received formal recognition in the Peace of Stockholm, 1720.

suspension of the right of election to the Parliament and the like, are in some circumstances a natural and unavoidable consequence of the state of war.

The inhabitants of the occupied territory owe the same obedience to the organs of Government and administration of the conqueror as they owed before the occupation to their own. An act of disobedience cannot be excused by reference to the laws or commands of one's own Government; even so an attempt to remain associated with the old Government or to act in agreement with it is punishable. On the other hand, the provisional Government can demand nothing which can be construed as an offense against one's own Fatherland or as a direct or indirect participation in the war.

The inhabitants must obey.

The civil and criminal jurisdiction continues in force as before. The introduction of an extraordinary administration of justice—martial law and courts-martial—is therefore only to take place if the behavior of the inhabitants makes it necessary. The latter are, in this respect, to be cautioned, and any such introduction is to be made known by appropriate means. The courts-martial must base any sentence on the fundamental laws of justice, after they have first impartially examined, however summarily, the facts and have allowed the accused a free defense.

Martial Law.

The conqueror can, as administrator of the country and its Government, depose or appoint officials. He can put on their oath the civil servants, who continue to act, as regards the scrupulous discharge of their duties. But to compel officials to continue in office against their will does not appear to be in the interest of the army of occupation. Transgressions by officials are punished by the laws of their country, but an abuse of their position to the prejudice of the army of occupation will be punished by martial law.

Also judicial officers can be deposed if they permit themselves to oppose publicly the instructions of the provisional Government. Thus it would not have been possible, if the occupation of Lorraine in the year 1870–71 had been protracted, to avoid deposing the whole bench of Judges at Nancy and substituting German Judges, since they could not agree with the German demands in regard to the promulgation of sentence.[2]

Fiscal Policy.

The financial administration of the occupied territory passes into the hands of the conqueror. The taxes are raised in the preexisting fashion. Any increase in them due to the war is enforced in the form of "War levies." Out of the revenue of the taxes the costs of the administration are to be

---

[2] The German administration desired that, as hitherto, justice should be administered in the name of the Emperor (Napoleon III). The Court, on the contrary, desired, after the revolution of September 4th, 1870, to use the formula: "In the name of the French Republic." The Court no longer recognized the Emperor as Sovereign, the German authorities did not yet recognize the Republic. Finally the Court, unfortunately for the inhabitants, ceased its activities. The proper solution would have been, according to Bluntschli (547), either the use of a neutral formula, as, for example, "In the name of the law," or the complete omission of the superfluous formula.

defrayed, as, generally speaking, the foundations of the State property are to be kept undisturbed. Thus the domains, forests, woodlands, public buildings and the like, although utilized, leased, or let out, are not to be sold or rendered valueless by predatory management. On the other hand it is permitted to apply all surplus from the revenues of administration to the use of the conqueror.

The same thing holds good of railways, telegraphs, telephones, canals, steamships, submarine cables and similar things; the conqueror has the right of sequestration, of use and of appropriation of any receipts, as against which it is incumbent upon him to keep them in good repair.

If these establishments belong to private persons, then he has indeed the right to use them to the fullest extent; on the other hand he has not the right to sequestrate the receipts. As regards the right of annexing the rolling-stock of the railways, the opinions of authoritative teachers of the law of nations differ from one another. Whilst one section regard all rolling-stock as one of the most important war resources of the enemy's State, and in consequence claim for the conqueror the right of unlimited sequestration, even if the railways belonged to private persons or private companies,[3] on the other hand the other section incline to a

---

[3] Stein, *Revue* 17, Declaration of Brussels, Article 6.

milder interpretation of the question, in that they start from the view that the rolling-stock forms, along with the immovable material of the railways, an inseparable whole, and that one without the other is worthless and is therefore subject to the same laws as to appropriation.[4] The latter view in the year 1871 found practical recognition in so far as the rolling-stock captured in large quantities by the Germans on the French railways was restored at the end of the war; a corresponding regulation was also adopted by the Hague Conference in 1899.

Occupation must be real not fictitious.

These are the chief principles for the administration of an occupied country or any portion of it. From them emerges quite clearly on the one hand the duties of the population, but also on the other the limits of the power of the conqueror. But the enforcement of all these laws presupposes the actual occupation of the enemy's territory and the possibility of really carrying them out.[5] So-called "fictitious occupation," such as frequently occurred in the eighteenth century and only existed in a declaration of the claimant, without the country concerned being actually occupied, are no longer recognized by influential authorities on the law of nations as valid. If the conqueror is com-

---

[4] *Manuel* 51; Moynier, *Revue*, XIX, 165.

[5] Article 42 of the Hague Regulations runs: "Territory is considered to be occupied when it is placed as a matter of fact under the authority of the hostile army. The occupation extends only to territories where that authority is established and capable of being exercised."

pelled by the vicissitudes of war to quit an occupied territory, or if it is voluntarily given up by
him, then his military sovereignty immediately
ceases and the old State authority of itself again
steps into its rights and duties.

PART III

USAGES OF WAR AS REGARDS NEUTRAL STATES

By the neutrality of a State is to be understood non-participation in the war by third parties; the duly attested intention not to participate in the conduct of the war either in favor of, or to the prejudice of, either one of the two belligerents. This relationship gives rise in the case of the neutral State to certain rights but also to fixed duties. These are not laid down by international regulations or international treaties; we have therefore here also to do with "Usages of War." *What neutrality means.*

What is principally required of a neutral State is equal treatment of both belligerents. If, therefore, the neutral State could support the belligerents at all, it would have to give its support in equal measure to both parties. As this is quite impossible and as one of the two parties—and probably every one of them—would regard itself as injured in any case, it therefore follows as a practical and empirical principle "not to support the two [*i.e.*, either or both] belligerents is the fundamental condition of neutrality." *A neutral cannot be all things to all men; therefore he must be nothing to any of them.*

But this principle would scarcely be maintained in its entirety, because in that case the trade and *But there are limits to this detachment.*

117

intercourse of the neutral State would in some circumstances be more injured than that of the belligerents themselves. But no State can be compelled to act against its own vital interests, therefore it is necessary to limit the above principle as follows: "No neutral State can support the belligerents as far as military operations are concerned. This principle sounds very simple and lucid, its content is, however, when closely considered very ambiguous and in consequence the danger of dissensions between neutral and belligerent States is very obvious."

In the following pages the chief duties of neutral States are to be briefly developed. It is here assumed that neutrality is not to be regarded as synonymous with indifference and impartiality towards the belligerents and the continuance of the war. As regards the expression of partizanship all that is required of neutral States is the observance of international courtesies; so long as these are observed there is no occasion for interference.

Duties of the neutral.

The chief duties of neutral States are to be regarded as:

Belligerents must be warned off.

1. The territory of neutral States is available for none of the belligerents for the conduct of its military operations.[1] The Government of the

---

[1] The passage of French troops through Prussian territory October, 1805, was a contempt of Prussian neutrality.—The moment the Swiss Government permitted the Allies to march through its territory in the year 1814, it thereby renounced the rights of a neutral State.—In the Franco-Prussian War the Prussian Government complained of the behavior of Luxemburg in not stopping a passage *en masse* of fugitive French soldiers after the fall of Metz through the territory of the Grand Duchy.

neutral State has therefore, once War is declared, to prevent the subjects of both parties from marching through it; it has likewise to prevent the laying out of factories and workshops for the manufacture of War requisites for one or other of the parties. Also the organization of troops and the assembling of "Freelances" on the territory of neutral States is not allowed by the law of nations.[2]

2. If the frontiers of the neutral State match with those of the territory where the War is being waged, its Government must take care to occupy its own frontiers in sufficient strength to prevent any portions of the belligerent Armies stepping across it with the object of marching through or of recovering after a Battle, or of withdrawing from War captivity. Every member of the belligerent Army who trespasses upon the territory of the neutral State is to be disarmed and to be put out of action till the end of the War. If whole detachments step across, they must likewise be dealt

The neutral must guard its inviolable frontiers. It must intern the Trespassers.

---

[2] The considerable reenforcement of the Servian Army in the year 1876 by Russian Freelances was an open violation of neutrality, the more so as the Government gave the officers permission, as the Emperor himself confessed later to the English Ambassador in Livadia. The English Foreign Enlistment Act of 1870, Art. 4,* forbids all English subjects during a war in which England remains neutral, to enter the army or the navy of a belligerent State, or the enlistment for the purpose, without the express permission of the Government. Similarly the American law of 1818. The United States complained energetically during the Crimean War of English recruiting on their territory.

*[This Act applies to British subjects wherever they may be, and it also applies to aliens, but only if they enlisted or promoted enlistment on British territory. For a full discussion of the scope of the Act see *R. v. Jameson* (1896), 2 Q.B. 425.—J. H. M.]

with. They are, indeed, not prisoners of War, but, nevertheless, are to be prevented from returning to the seat of War. A discharge before the end of the War would presuppose a particular arrangement of all parties concerned.

If a convention to cross over is concluded, then, according to the prevalent usages of War, a copy of the conditions is to be sent to the Victor.[3] If the troops passing through are taking with them prisoners of War, then these are to be treated in like fashion. Obviously, the neutral State can later demand compensation for the maintenance and care of the troops who have crossed over, or it can keep back War material as a provisional payment. Material which is liable to be spoilt, or the keeping of which would be disproportionately costly, as, for example, a considerable number of horses, can be sold, and the net proceeds set off against the cost of internment.

Unneutral service.

3. A neutral State can support no belligerent by furnishing military resources of any kind whatsoever, and is bound to prevent as much as possible the furnishing of such wholesale on the part of its subjects. The ambiguity of

---

[3] At the end of August, 1870, some French detachments, without its being known, marched through Belgian territory; others in large numbers fled after the Battle at Sedan to Belgium, and were there disarmed. In February, 1871, the hard-pressed French Army of the East crossed into Switzerland and were there likewise disarmed.

the notion *"Kriegsmittel"* has often led to complications. The most indispensable means for the conduct of a War is money. For this very reason it is difficult to prevent altogether the support of one or other party by citizens of neutral States, since there will always be Bankers who, in the interest of the State in whose success they put confidence, and whose solvency in the case of a defeat they do not doubt, will promote a loan. Against this nothing can be said from the point of view of the law of nations; rather the Government of a country cannot be made responsible for the actions of individual citizens, it could only accept responsibility if business of this kind was done by Banks immediately under the control of the State or on public Stock Exchanges.

The "sinews of war"— loans to belligerents.

It is otherwise with the supply of contraband of war, that is to say, such things as are supplied to a belligerent for the immediate support of war as being warlike resources and equipment. These may include:

Contraband of War.

   (*a*) Weapons of war (guns, rifles, sabers, etc., ammunition, powder and other explosives, and military conveyances, etc.).

   (*b*) Any materials out of which this kind of war supplies can be manufactured, such as saltpeter, sulphur, coal, leather, and the like.

(c) Horses and mules.

(d) Clothing and equipment (such as uniforms of all kinds, cooking utensils, leather straps, and footwear).

(e) Machines, motor-cars, bicycles, telegraphic apparatus, and the like.

Good business.

All these things are indispensable for the conduct of war, their supply in great quantities means a proportionately direct support of the belligerent. On the other hand, it cannot be left out of account that many of the above-mentioned objects also pertain to the peaceable needs of men, *i.e.*, to the means without which the practise of any industry would be impossible, and the feeding of great masses of the population doubtful. The majority of European States are, even in time of peace, dependent on the importation from other countries of horses, machines, coal, and the like, even as they are upon that of corn, preserved foods, store cattle, and other necessaries of life. The supply of such articles by subjects of a neutral State may, therefore, be just as much an untainted business transaction and pacific, as a support of a belligerent. The question whether the case amounts to the one or the other is therefore to be judged each time upon its merits. In practise, the following conceptions have developed themselves in the course of time:

(a) The purchase of necessaries of life, store cattle, preserved foods, etc., in the territory of a neutral, even if it is meant, as a matter of common knowledge, for the revictualing of the Army, is not counted a violation of neutrality, provided only that such purchases are equally open to both parties.

Foodstuffs.

(b) The supply of contraband of war, in small quantities, on the part of subjects of a neutral State to one of the belligerents is, so far as it bears the character of a peaceable business transaction and not that of an intentional aid to the war, not a violation of neutrality. No Government can be expected to prevent it in isolated and trivial cases, since it would impose on the States concerned quite disproportionate exertions, and on their citizens countless sacrifices of money and time. He who supplies a belligerent with contraband does so on his own account and at his own peril, and exposes himself to the risk of Prize.[4]

Contraband on a small scale.

---

[4] In the negotiations in 1793, as to the neutrality of North America in the Anglo-French War, Jefferson declared: "The right of the citizens to fashion, sell, and export arms cannot be suspended by a foreign war, but American citizens pursue it on their own account and at their own risk."—Bluntschll, sec. 425 (2). Similarly in the famous treaty between Prussia and the United States of September 10th, 1785, it was expressly fixed in Article 13 that if one of the two

continued on page 124

And on a large scale.

(c) The supply of war resources on a large scale stands in a different position. Undoubtedly this presents a case of actual promotion of a belligerent's cause, and generally of a warlike succor. If, therefore, a neutral State wishes to place its detachment from the war beyond doubt, and to exhibit it clearly, it must do its utmost to prevent such supplies being delivered. The instructions to the Customs authorities must thus be clearly and precisely set out, that on the one hand they notify the will of the Government to set their face against such wanton bargains with all their might, but that on the other, they do not arbitrarily restrict and cripple the total home trade.

The practise differs.

In accordance with this view many neutral States, such as Switzerland, Belgium, Japan, etc., did, during the Franco-Prussian War, forbid all supply or transit of arms to a belligerent, whilst England and the United States put no kind of obstacles whatsoever in the way of the traffic in arms, and contented themselves with drawing the attention of their commercial classes to the fact that arms were contra-

---

States was involved in war and the other State should remain neutral, the traders of the latter should not be prevented from selling arms and munitions to the enemy of the other. Thus the contraband articles were not to be confiscated, but the merchants were to be paid the value of their goods by the belligerent who had seized them. This arrangement was, however, not inserted in the newer treaties between Prussia and the Union in 1799 and 1828.

band, and were therefore exposed to capture on the part of the injured belligerent.[5]

It is evident, therefore, that the views of this particular relation of nations with each other still need clearing up, and that the unanimity which one would desire on this question does not exist.

4. The neutral State may allow the passage or transport of wounded or sick through its territory without thereby violating its neutrality; it has, however, to watch that hospital trains do not carry with them either war personnel or war material with the exception of that which is necessary for the care of the sick.[6]

Who may pass—the Sick and the Wounded.

5. The passage or transport of prisoners of war through neutral territory is, on the other hand, not to be allowed, since this would be an open favoring of the belligerent who happened to be in a position to make prisoners of war on a

Who may not pass— Prisoners of War.

---

[5] In the exchange of despatches between England and Germany which arose out of the English deliveries of arms, the English Minister, Lord Granville, declares, in reply to the complaints of the German Ambassador in London, Count Bernstorff, that this behavior is authorized by the preexisting practise, but adds that "with the progress of civilization the obligations of neutrals have become more stringent, and declares his readiness to consult with other nations as to the possibility of introducing in concert more stringent rules, although his expectations of a practical result are, having regard to the declarations of the North-American Government, not very hopeful." President Grant had, it is true, already in the Neutrality Proclamation of August 22nd, 1870, declared the trade in contraband in the United States to be permitted, but had uttered a warning that the export of the same over sea was forbidden by international law. He had later expressly forbidden the American arsenal administration to sell arms to a belligerent, an ordinance which was of course self-evident and was observed even in England, but he did not attempt to prevent dealers taking advantage of the public sale of arms out of the State arsenals to buy them for export to the French.

[6] Belgium allowed itself, in August, 1870, owing to the opposition of France, to be talked into forbidding the transport of wounded after the Battle of Sedan, through Belgian territory, and out of excessive caution interpreted its
continued on page 126

large scale, while his own railways, water high-
ways, and other means of transport remained
free for exclusively military purposes.

These are the most important duties of neutral
States so far as land warfare is concerned. If they
are disregarded by the neutral State itself, then it
has to give satisfaction or compensation to the belligerent who is prejudiced thereby. This case may
also occur if the Government of the neutral State,
with the best intentions to abstain from proceedings which violate neutrality, has, through domestic or foreign reasons, not the power to make its
intentions good. If, for example, one of the two
belligerents by main force marches through the
territory of a neutral State and this State is not in a
position to put an end to this violation of its neutrality, then the other belligerent has the right to
engage the enemy on the hitherto neutral territory.

Rights of
the neutral.

The duties of neutral States involve corresponding rights, such as:

The neutral
has the
right to be
left alone.

1. The neutral State has the right to be regarded
as still at peace with the belligerents as with
others.

---

decree of August 27th as amounting to a prohibition of the transport even of
individual wounded. The French protest was based on the contention that by
the transport of wounded through Belgium, the military communication of the
enemy with Germany was relieved from a serious hindrance." On such a
ground—thinks Bluntschli (p. 434)—"one might set one's face against the
transport of large numbers but not the transport of individuals. These considerations of humanity should decide."

2. The belligerent States have to respect the inviolability of the neutral and the undisturbed
   exercise of its sovereignty in its home affairs,
   to abstain from any attack upon the same,
   even if the necessity of war should make such
   an attack desirable. Neutral States, therefore,
   possess also the right of asylum for single
   members or adherents of the belligerent Powers, so far as no favor to one or other of them
   is thereby implied. Even the reception of a
   smaller or larger detachment of troops which
   is fleeing from pursuit does not give the pur-
   suer the right to continue his pursuit across
   the frontier of the neutral territory. It is the
   business of the neutral State to prevent troops
   crossing over in order to reassemble in the
   chosen asylum, reform, and sally out to a new
   attack.

   Neutral territory is sacred.

3. If the territory of a neutral State is trespassed
   upon by one of the belligerent parties for the
   purpose of its military operations, then this
   State has the right to proceed against this violation of its territory with all the means in its
   power and to disarm the trespassers. If the
   trespass has been committed on the orders of
   the Army Staff, then the State concerned is
   bound to give satisfaction and compensation;
   if it has been committed on their own responsibility, then the individual offenders can be
   punished as criminals. If the violation of the

   *The neutral may resist a violation of its terri-
   tory "with all the means in its power."*

neutral territory is due to ignorance of its
frontiers and not to evil intention, then the
neutral State can demand the immediate
removal of the wrong, and can insist on necessary measures being taken to prevent a repetition of such contempts.

Neutrality
is
presumed.

4. Every neutral State can, so long as it itself
keeps faith, demand that the same respect
shall be paid to it as in time of peace. It is entitled to the presumption that it will observe
strict neutrality and will not make use of any
declarations or other transactions as a cloak
for an injustice against one belligerent in favor
of the other, or will use them indifferently for
both. This is particularly important in regard
to Passes, Commissions, and credentials
issued by a neutral State.[7]

The
property of
neutrals.

5. The property of the neutral State, as also that
of its citizens, is, even if it lies within the seat
of war, to be respected so far as the necessity
of war allows. It can obviously be attacked
and even destroyed in certain circumstances
by the belligerents, but only if complete compensation be afterwards made to the injured
owners. Thus—to make this clear by an example from the year 1870—the capture and sink-
ing of six English colliers at Duclaix was both

---

[7] Dr. A. W. Heffter, *Das Europäische Völkerrecht der Gegenwart* (7th ed.),
1882, p. 320.

justified and necessary on military grounds, but it was, for all that, a violent violation of English property, for which on the English side compensation was demanded, and on the German side was readily forthcoming.

6. Neutral States may continue to maintain diplomatic intercourse with the belligerent Powers undisturbed, so far as military measures do not raise obstacles in the way of it.

Diplomatic intercourse.

THE END

INDEX